The Little Book Of

CLOUD COMPUTING

2013 Edition

Including Coverage of Big Data Tools

Lars Nielsen

2013
New Street Communications, LLC
Wickford, RI

newstreetcommunications.com

Published January 2013 by
New Street Communications, LLC
Wickford, Rhode Island
newstreetcommunications.com

Contents

Vincent Van Gogh

Cloud Drawing, Pencil

Saint-Rémy: March - April, 1890

Original in the Van Gogh Museum

Amsterdam, The Netherlands

Introduction

A leading programmer and systems administrator with more than 30 years experience, Lars Nielsen here provides an incisive yet user-friendly introduction to Cloud Computing – that vital, ubiquitous resource which offers so much to organizations in the way of scaled business computing efficiency and economy.

The research firm Gartner projects that revenue for Cloud services will approach $152.1 billion by 2014.

"One factor that's driving demand for Cloud Computing is the explosive growth of data," comments Ana Cantu of Dell. "According to projections by Century Link, by 2015, the world will see a four-fold increase in the amount of data being created and replicated. And once all of that data comes into being, you need a way to store it all securely and allow end-users to access it efficiently." And that demand is what's putting a silver lining on the Cloud.

Then there is also the fact of energy efficiency. As Cantu reminds us: "According to a recent Carbon Disclosure Project report, companies that streamline operations to improve IT performance will not only reduce capital expenditures but they'll shrink energy consumption and carbon emissions. The group estimated that, by 2020, U.S. organizations that move to the Cloud could save $12.3

billion in energy costs and the equivalent of 200 million barrels of oil."

But still, Cloud Computing remains in its infancy.

71% of technology experts participating in a recent Pew Research survey expressed complete agreement with the following statement: "By 2020, most people won't do their work with software running on a general-purpose PC. Instead, they will work in Internet-based applications such as Google Docs, and in applications run from smartphones. Aspiring application developers will develop for smartphone vendors and companies that provide Internet-based applications, because most innovative work will be done in that domain, instead of designing applications that run on a PC operating system."

Peter Coffee, VP and Head of Platform Research at Salesforce.com, believes that the next phase of Cloud Computing development will involve several key factors. Coffee says that surging volume of externally originating data (e.g., social nets) will drive more companies to Cloud-based analytics. He also suggests that file-based models of collaboration will give way to Cloud-based, conversational models like Chatter where file location is irrelevant. Further, he speculates that continued scarcity of IT skills – despite still-high general unemployment – will discourage complex 'private Cloud' schemes.

Christian Reilly, Manager of Global Systems Engineering at Bechtel, insists that in short order traditional enterprises will begin to accept that there is no magic formula for moving their incumbent LoB applications "to the Cloud" *en masse*. "We will see enlightened enterprises (i.e. those who have already invested time and effort in portfolio identification and consolidation) execute on a multi-faceted deployment and operations strategy for best-shoring their application workloads."

Another prediction from Reilly: "Private Cloud solutions will continue to lead the way in this as organizations continue to look for further efficiencies and increased agility to complement their initial server virtualization investments – this combined with deploying 'capable' applications and some new workloads to public Cloud services."

And just one more: "[The next year or so] will bring an uptake in interest in Cloud concierge services where the emergence of new marketplaces for offering and acquiring Cloud services will appeal to many forward-thinking CIOs as they transition from solution providers to service aggregators. Initially, we will see this develop in 'carrier-neutral' data center facilities where typical cross-connect services begin to evolve to higher value services, connecting customers to providers through a global offering."

Of course, virtually all pundits agree that in 2013 Big Data will loom larger and larger in Cloud development, and Lars Nielsen has taken pains in this new edition of *The Little Book of Cloud Computing* to address the ever-enlarging shelf of tools and platforms being made available by leading Cloud service providers to enable and facilitate Big Data analytics.

Big Data, after all, is at center-stage these days.

Per McKinsey & Company: "The amount of data in our world has been exploding, and analyzing large data sets (so-called Big Data) will become a key basis of competition, underpinning new waves of productivity growth, innovation, and consumer surplus ... Leaders in every sector will have to grapple with the implications of Big Data, not just a few data-oriented managers. The increasing volume and detail of information captured by enterprises, the rise of multimedia, social media, and the Internet of Things will fuel exponential growth in data for the foreseeable future."

McKinsey: "There are five broad ways in which using Big Data can create value. First, Big Data can unlock significant value by making information transparent and usable at much higher frequency. Second, as organizations create and store more transactional data in digital form, they can collect more accurate and detailed performance information on everything from product inventories to sick days, and therefore expose variability and boost performance. Leading companies are using data collection and analysis to conduct controlled experiments to make better management decisions; others are using data for basic low-frequency forecasting to high-frequency nowcasting to adjust their business levers just in time. Third, Big Data allows ever-narrower segmentation of customers and therefore much more precisely tailored products or services. Fourth, sophisticated analytics can substantially improve decision-making. Finally, Big Data can be used to improve the development of the next generation of products and services. For instance, manufacturers are using data obtained from sensors embedded in products to create innovative after-sales service offerings such as proactive maintenance (preventive measures that take place before a failure occurs or is even noticed)."

"Big Data is an 'umbrella' term that is commonly used to refer to a number of advanced data storage, access and analytics technologies aimed at handling high volume and/or fast moving data in a variety of scenarios." So writes industry analyst Colin Beveridge. "These typically involve low signal-to-noise ratios, such as social media sentiment monitoring, or log file analysis, to mention just a couple."

Beveridge continues: "Given the number of vendors jumping onto the bandwagon, it's hard to pin down where the Big Data discussion stops and starts."

Industry pundit Gil Press: "Consider this scenario: By the end of this decade, a number of established and emerging enterprises will become Big Data-driven entities, expanding beyond their narrowly defined 'industries' to become full-fledged IT players, working with or competing with traditional IT vendors to develop and deliver IT solutions for a wide range of customers. ... Digitization has made data an indispensable resource for any enterprise, second only to people. Big Data is about applying this resource in the most optimal way. This shift in emphasis may well mean a significant change in how IT is developed, sold, and bought."

Writing for *Forbes*, Tom Groenfeldt notes: "To get the greatest business value from Big Data, companies are looking for multi-skilled experts who understand programming, large-scale mathematics, statistics and business. They call this new role a Data Scientist. ... Commercial demand is apt to rise sharply within the next few years as social media, sensors, and other new data generators make petabytes a routine part of business analytics. Universities are busy creating Data Scientist programs while existing data-intensive firms are creating their own, even if they don't use the label, by training their current analysts, quants, Excel jockeys and computer-savvy MBAs in some Big Data skills like Hadoop."

Writing for *InformationWeek*, Doug Henschen tells us: "Excitement around Hadoop has been building since its release as an open source distributed data processing platform five years ago. But within the last 18 months, Hadoop has taken off, gaining customers, commercial support options, and dozens of integrations from database and data-integration software vendors. The top three commercial database suppliers – Oracle, IBM, and Microsoft – have adopted Hadoop. ... Will Hadoop turn out to be as significant as SQL, introduced more than 30 years ago? Hadoop is often tagged as a technology exclusively for unstructured data. By combining scalability, flexibility, and low cost, it has become the default choice for Web giants like AOL and ComScore that are dealing with large-scale clickstream analysis and ad targeting scenarios."

Henschen continues: "But Hadoop is headed for wider use. It's applicable for all types of data and destined to go beyond clickstream and sentiment analysis. For example, SunGard, a hosting and application service provider for small and midsize companies, plans to introduce a cloud-based managed service aimed at helping financial services companies experiment with Hadoop-based MapReduce processing. And software-as-a-service startup Tidemark recently introduced a cloud-based performance management application that will use MapReduce to bring mixed data sources into product and financial planning scenarios."

McKinsey: "The use of Big Data will become a key basis of competition and growth for individual firms. From the standpoint of competitiveness and the potential capture of value, all companies need to take Big Data seriously. In most industries, established competitors and new entrants alike will leverage data-driven strategies to innovate, compete, and capture value from deep and up-to-real-time information ... The use of Big Data will underpin new waves of productivity growth and consumer surplus. For example, we estimate that a retailer using Big Data to the full has the potential to increase its operating margin by more than 60 percent. Big Data offers considerable benefits to consumers as well as to companies and organizations. For instance, services enabled by personal-location data can allow consumers to capture $600 billion in economic surplus."

*

Let me close with one important word for readers of this book's previous 2011 and 2012 editions. You will notice that the first two chapters have undergone very little in the way revision. Quite simply, the "Basics" of Cloud Computing, just like the "Technology and Business Fundamentals" of Cloud Computing do not change very much from year to year. The balance of this book has, however, been radically revised and greatly expanded and updated to encompass the very latest developments related to this fast-changing technology.

Edward Renehan
Managing Director
New Street Communications, LLC
Wickford, RI

The Basics

Cloud Computing in Brief

What is a Cloud? A Cloud is a floating mass of water droplets (or sometimes frozen crystals of ice) suspended above the earth's atmosphere. It is also – more importantly for our purpose here – a metaphor for the Internet.

Cloud Computing, in turn, is computing which leverages the Internet as a tool through which remote computers share memory, processing, network capacity, software and other IT services on-demand. The Cloud paradigm allows businesses to pay-as-they-go in a "utility computing" manner while using only that amount of computer capacity which they need at any given moment. Thus organizations can avoid a massive one-time investment in hardware platforms, operating systems, memory and applications licenses – all of which they may or may not fully use over time, or which may conversely in the long-term prove inadequate, requiring costly upgrades.

In mid-2008, the Gartner Group forecast that Cloud Computing would soon "shape the relationship among consumers of IT services, those who use IT services and those who sell them" and observed that organizations were "switching from company-owned hardware and software assets to per-use service-based models." Gartner also predicted that the "projected shift to Cloud Computing ... will result in dramatic growth in IT products in some areas and significant reductions in other areas." In the years since, we've seen that the Gartner Group forecast was spot-on.

Via Cloud Computing, many share the resources, and the expense, of a pool of configurable computing resources, thus driving down costs through a system of multi-tenancy. This includes applications, which are packaged and offered in a "Software as a Service" (SaaS) paradigm. Likewise the Cloud offers "Platform as a Service" (PaaS) and "Infrastructure as a Service" (IaaS). SaaS demands the least in technical expertise from the client. IaaS demands the most.

In essence, Cloud Computing is the broadest possible extension of the classic client-server computing model. But in this extension, because of the ubiquitous nature of the Cloud, the idea of a specific "server" being contacted goes by the wayside. The "server" itself becomes a virtualized abstraction, while the main object of the transaction – the resource being "served" – remains anything but an abstraction, whether this resource be database processing, memory (data storage), applications tools, or what have you.

Overall, Cloud Computing is characterized by five main attributes: on-demand self-service, extremely broad network access, resource pooling, unlimited and prompt scalability, and measured (metered) service.

For those who prefer a more formal definition of Cloud Computing, we have this from The National Institute of Standards and Technology: "Cloud Computing is a model for enabling convenient, on-demand network access to a shared pool of configurable computing resources (e.g., networks, servers, storage, applications, and services) that can be rapidly provisioned and released with minimal management effort or service provider interaction."

Cloud Computing can be scaled to match any organizational need. Private, proprietary Clouds can be set up to be shared by divisions of a single organization, or by a few allied organizations. Public Clouds, meanwhile, are open to all who are willing to pay for services rendered.

In the immediate future, it is likely that many organizations of substantial size will wind up with a mixed IT environment incorporating both types of Cloud along with non-Cloud systems and applications – many of these legacies from the pre-Cloud era – in a hybrid Cloud model.

Business Benefits

Location-independent and device-independent, Cloud Computing has special appeal in this day when organizations themselves are so widely dispersed, with personnel who need to make many and various demands from company data resources via wireless while on the go, or from remote offices, and often needing to conference in the same manner.

At the same time, Cloud Computing enables organizations to divest themselves of the problems, capital expenses and human resource overhead that would otherwise be involved in the maintenance of dedicated networks, data banks, servers and processors. By reliance on a Cloud, your organization for the most part abdicates responsibility for necessary software, operating system and hardware upgrades, and other standard maintenance tasks. (When you own a home, it is up to you to manage the headaches and costs of replacing the roof. When you rent a home, it is up to the landlord. And unlike a home, computing capacity never goes up in dollar value, only down.)

Also worth keeping in mind is the fact that responsibility for the pricey process of electronic recycling (a necessary part of each and every hardware upgrade) resides with the Cloud provider.

With regard to energy usage and the Cloud, and the impact on a firm's carbon footprint, Microsoft's Chief Environmental Strategist Rob Bernard recently made this startling but accurate claim: "For an enterprise company, moving things like Exchange or Outlook over to our [Cloud] services ended up in a net reduction in energy of about 30 percent ... and a 30 percent reduction in carbon.

For a small business the number was even higher: 90 percent energy savings."

Bottom line: IT-based capital and staff expenditures drop dramatically for organizations leveraging Cloud resources, leaving only elastic operational IT expenditures on the balance sheet, these scaling with the ebb and flow of an organization's real usage.

Big Data Ability

Many enterprises are turning more and more to large repositories of corporate and external data to uncover trends, statistics, and other actionable information. These ubiquitous data sets, along with their related tools, platforms, and analytics, are generally referred to as "Big Data."

In addition to providing a research boon, Big Data fills another vital need of today's businesses. In order to comply with state and federal government regulations, as well as to meet the needs of e-discovery in the face of potential litigation, organizations increasingly face the need to maintain staggeringly large amounts of structured and unstructured data – everything from transaction records to employee tweets to regulatory filings.

Where to find a cost-effective platform that can store and access (and, if need be, analyze) massive data? Where to find a highly-scalable platform able to support not only

14

storage technologies but also query languages, analytics tools, content analysis tools, and transport infrastructures? Of course. You've guessed it. The Cloud.

Clouds

John Singer Sargent

Circa 1896

Original in the Metropolitan Museum of Art

New York, New York

Technology and Business Fundamentals

The Cloud Pyramid

The basic architecture of the Cloud is simple to illustrate. In what is called the "Cloud Pyramid," the resources of the Cloud can be visualized as three key segments: Cloud infrastructure at the bottom, Cloud platforms in the middle, and Cloud applications at the top.

Apps
Platform
Cloud Infrastructure

At the apps level of a Cloud, client enterprises are served fully functioning Software as a Service (SaaS) resources, with little need for programming on the part of the client. The client need not worry about the details of creating applications, building/maintaining platforms or over-seeing the details of infrastructure (physical data centers). Clients who purchase SaaS Cloud resources are, for the most part, acquiring turn-key access to standing computer tools just waiting to receive their data and begin processing.

At the platform level, client enterprises are served Platform as a Service (PaaS) resources. Clients purchasing PaaS resources abdicate the responsibility for platform construction/maintenance and the maintenance of infrastructure to the Cloud supplier, but they take upon themselves the task of either building their own custom applications or else installing apps supplied by third parties, and making sure they work well in concert. PaaS support offerings will usually include tools for application design, development, testing, deployment and hosting as well as services such as team collaboration, web service integration (and marshalling), along with database integration, security, scalability, storage, persistence, state management, application versioning, application instrumentation and developer community facilitation.

Lastly, client enterprises accessing the Cloud in an Infrastructure as a Service (IaaS) paradigm take it upon themselves to build/maintain their own platforms and applications. These clients are basically just purchasing raw computing capacity and storage.

Differentiating Public, Private and Hybrid Cloud Environments

When most people speak of Cloud Computing, they generally mean a "public Cloud." In a public Cloud a provider such as Amazon or Google makes computing resources (such as processing power, memory or storage) publicly available over the internet. In a public Cloud, the pay-as-you go model is present in its purest form, and resources are shared between all subscribers. Public Clouds typically run on open-source software to facilitate the movement of vast amounts of data. However, an increasing number of software companies (including Microsoft and Oracle) are beginning to provide Cloud infrastructures utilizing proprietary software.

Public Clouds are generally perceived – to an increasing extent, unfairly, as shall be shown in a later chapter – to be insecure environments where an organization's data is liable to theft, spying or destruction. This perception has helped two other types of computing Clouds rise in popularity: the private Cloud and the hybrid Cloud.

The term "private Cloud" refers to privately-held, discrete computing infrastructures that have capabilities similar to a Cloud but are not shared by diverse organizations. Although this paradigm eliminates many of the cost-benefits of Cloud Computing, it still allows for virtualization to simulate resource allocation, and therefore can save on at least some costs while also assuring an impregnable – albeit pricey – operating environment.

Of increasing popularity is the hybrid Cloud, which allows for most of the cost-savings associated with public Clouds, while also offering proprietary security. In a hybrid Cloud, a significant amount of processing and data storage gets transacted on a public Cloud, and the balance in a private Cloud. Most organizations have sensitive and non-sensitive information and applications. Not all data and not all operations need be bullet-proof. In most hybrid Clouds, the database servers containing sensitive proprietary information are kept on a private Cloud, while a public Cloud is used for everything else.

API Interface

The Application Programming Interface (API) is the key to Cloud Computing. It is the API which enables client machines to "interface" with Cloud software. Without the API, there is no Cloud Computing

Most Cloud Computing implementations use Representation State Transfer-based (REST-based) APIs.

REST software architecture, principally designed to help implement distributed hypermedia systems (ala the World Wide Web), was first elucidated in 2000 by Roy Fielding, a primary early shaper of the Hypertext Transfer Protocol (HTTP). (Like other systems conforming to the REST architecture, the Web is sometimes described as being "RESTful.") Indeed, REST was developed in tandem with HTTP; each is integrally involved with the other.

The primary function of REST is to control and modulate the innumerable interactions between those origin servers, gateways, proxies and clients which inhabit, inform and define the Cloud while at the same time setting no arbitrary limitations on these actors. Think of REST as a policing mechanism which allows traffic to go and behave where and how it will, but always in an orderly manner.

The Cloud and the UNIX Paradigm

When we speak of Cloud architecture we are actually referring to the multiple software systems employed to enable Cloud processing. These elegant, efficient systems are "Cloud components." These components communicate and collaborate via the API. Thus Cloud architecture can be seen as deriving from the classic UNIX paradigm: Multiple specialized programs, each with its own unique task, coming together in the Cloud, performing complex tasks far more expeditiously and economically than would be the case in any other architecture.

The front end of the Cloud architecture is that which is experienced by the client (aka, user). The front end includes the client's computer or proprietary network and those apps used to access the Cloud (often a web browser). The back end of the Cloud architecture is the abstracted haze of computers, servers and data storage devices which comprise the Cloud.

Cloud Service Providers

Numerous firms currently service the business of Cloud Computing. These firms, ranging from start-ups to industry monoliths such as IBM and Amazon and Google, provide the full range of services in metered, pay-as-you-go models for SaaS, PaaS and IaaS. They all offer detailed Service Level Agreements (SLAs) and meet key quality assurance benchmarks.

Cloud is about how you do computing, not where you do computing.

– Paul Maritz, Chief Strategy Officer, VMware/EMC Joint "Pivotal Initiative"

21

Amazon Web Services (AWS)

Including Amazon Elastic MapReduce (Amazon EMR), RedShift - a Data Warehouse Solution Bringing Analytics "To the Masses," - and PowerShell

Launched in 2006, Amazon Web Services (AWS) provides access to the same global computing infrastructure that represents the backbone to Amazon's multi-billion dollar transactional retail enterprise. Amazon's service is scalable, secure, and robust, and Amazon boasts a number of high-profile clients.

To date, Amazon is by far the leading brand in Cloud Computing. Per a report from the 451 Group, Amazon has "almost single-handedly moved Cloud Computing to the center of the IT innovation agenda." As William Fellows, principal analyst of the 451 Group, told the *Wall Street Journal's* Nick Clayton: "In terms of market share Amazon is Coke and there isn't yet a Pepsi."

"AWS is growing like crazy," reports *Bloomberg BusinessWeek*. "Although he won't cite exact numbers, [AWS head Andy] Jassy claims 'hundreds of thousands of customers' already use the service, ... In fact, a whole generation of Internet companies couldn't exist without it. Netflix's movie-streaming empire runs on it; Zynga, the social gaming company, uses it to handle sudden spikes in usage. AWS has become such a fact of life for Silicon Valley startups that venture capitalists actually hand out Amazon gift cards to entrepreneurs. Keeping up with the demand requires frantic expansion: Each day, Jassy's operation adds enough computing muscle to power one whole Amazon.com circa 2000, when it was a $2.8 billion business."

UBS Investment Research estimates AWS revenue could hit $2.5 billion in 2014.

Werner Vogels, Chief Technology Officer (CTO) of Amazon, emphasizes the strength of the "ecosystem" provided by AWS. "The Cloud is actually a very large collection of services. Think of everything as a service," says Vogels. Citing Alfred Korzybski, the early 20th century Polish scientist who famously said "The map is not the territory," Vogels emphasizes that the Cloud's ecosystem "is what defines the Cloud, rather than the infrastructure services underneath them." Vogel extolls a number of robust new services built by third parties atop the Amazon infrastructure, including BitNami, which builds open source software stacks as Amazon Machine Images; Aspera for software license management in the Cloud; Riverbed for accelerated file and data transfer; and SafeNet's DS3 three-tier authentication management. "Let a thousand platforms bloom ... It's still day one in the Cloud."

Like other web service providers, AWS empowers organizations to requisition elastic computer processing power and storage on demand via a range of IT infrastructure tools. IT personnel can choose from any number of development platforms and programming models. They control the resources consumed, and fit them into custom applications as they necessary. But they don't necessarily have to start from scratch. AWS offers a number of off-the-shelf solutions – strong SaaS tools – that can easily be plugged into applications. These include tools for managing databases (Amazon SimpleDB), queues (Amazon SQS), payments (Amazon FPS), and more – the very same tools Amazon has developed and deployed for its own sales operations.

As with all metered Cloud providers, with AWS you pay only for what you use. AWS clients can set themselves up with absolutely no up-front expenses and no long-term commitments. All AWS services can be used independently or deployed together to create a complete computing platform in the Cloud. These services include the following.

Amazon CloudFront enables high performance, globally distributed content delivery. Clients' applications can use Amazon CloudFront to distribute or stream content to users with low latency, high data transfer speeds, and seamless integration with Amazon S3.

Amazon Elastic Compute Cloud (Amazon EC2) provides resizable compute capacity in the Cloud. Clients define their own virtual Amazon EC2 environment with the operating system, services, databases, and application platform stack required for their hosted applications.

Amazon EC2 provides a full management console and APIs to compute resources.

Amazon Simple Queue Service (Amazon SQS) delivers a high performance, secure queuing system to reliably distribute work between application processes. Amazon SQS enables developers and businesses to move data between distributed components of their applications that perform different tasks without losing messages or requiring each component to be always available.

Amazon Simple Storage Service (Amazon S3) comprises a simple web services interface that can be used to store and retrieve large amounts of data, at any time, from anywhere on the web. It gives developers and businesses access to the same data storage infrastructure that Amazon uses to run its own global network of web sites.

Amazon Virtual Private Cloud (Amazon VPC) provides a secure and seamless bridge between a company's existing IT infrastructure and the AWS Cloud. Amazon VPC enables enterprises to connect their existing infrastructure to a set of isolated AWS compute resources via a Virtual Private Network (VPN) connection, and to extend their existing management capabilities such as security services, firewalls, and intrusion detection systems to include their AWS resources.

Amazon Elastic MapReduce (Amazon EMR) enables businesses, researchers, data analysts, data scientists and developers to cost-effectively process vast amounts of data. EMR empoys a hosted Hadoop framework running on the web-scale infrastructure of Amazon EC2 and Amazon S3.

Additional tools include *Redshift*, the *Alexa Web Information Service, AWS Identity and Access Management* (IAM) and *Amazon Simple Queue Service* (SQS).

More tools are to come. Speaking to Arik Hesseldahl of "All Things Digital," Adam Selipsky, vice president of Product Management and Developer Relations at Amazon Web Services, explains: "As fast as we knock out new services and features, the list of what our customers want from us continues to grow. I think that's because this is so new, and since we're replacing the data center, there's a lot of things built up over the decades that run in those data centers. There's going to be a long list of mission critical services that we need to bring up."

One of Amazon's coolest developments is the *Elastic Beanstalk*. As described by Amazon staff: "AWS *Elastic Beanstalk* is an even easier way for you to quickly deploy and manage applications in the AWS Cloud. You simply upload your application, and *Elastic Beanstalk* automatically handles the deployment details of capacity provisioning, load balancing, auto-scaling, and application health monitoring. At the same time, with *Elastic Beanstalk*, you retain full control over the AWS resources powering your application and can access the underlying resources at any time. *Elastic Beanstalk* leverages AWS services such as *Amazon EC2, Amazon S3, Amazon Simple Notification Service, Elastic Load Balancing*, and *Auto-Scaling* to deliver the same highly reliable, scalable, and cost-effective infrastructure that hundreds of thousands of businesses depend on today. AWS *Elastic Beanstalk* is easy to begin and impossible to outgrow."

Check Point Software Technologies Security via "Virtual Appliances"

"Security gateways in Cloud environments are equally as important as they are in on-premise locations; therefore, unifying their policies and reporting capabilities in a centralized way is critical to ensuring both the security and compliance mandates of enterprises worldwide," says Lawrence Pingree, research director at Gartner.

Under a new partnership announced early January 2012, AWS customers have Check Point Software Technologies' virtual security appliances built into their customized Cloud environments. AWS customers will be able to manage Check Point's virtual security gateways from the centralized management dashboard to apply security policies to the Cloud infrastructure. Virtual Appliance for Amazon Web Services offers customers access to more than 30 security applications, including a firewall, virtual private network, URL filtering, application control, intrusion prevention, mobile access, data loss prevention, antivirus and others.

Customers bring their own applications onto Amazon's Cloud infrastructure, and can use Check Point's line of virtual appliances to add their own layers of security on top of what is already in place. The customer picks and chooses between more than 30 software "blades," or security applications, in order to create the level of security they require.

Big Data and Data Science with AWS, Including Amazon EMR and Redshift

A bit more needs to be said about *Amazon Elastic MapReduce* (Amazon EMR). Data Scientists manipulating and mining "Big Data" located on AWS will find this indispensable. EMR allows professionals involved in the Data Science function to quickly provision as much capacity as necessary to carry-out data-intensive tasks for such functions as web indexing, data mining, log file analysis, data warehousing, machine learning, scientific simulation, financial analysis and research into bioinformatics. EMR provides a cost- and time-effective environment in which to crunch and analyze data without burning up budget-dollars on set-up, management or tuning of Hadoop clusters. EMR includes seamless integration with the MapR Distribution of Hadoop as well as the ability to run Hbase.

In addition to EMR, it is likely Amazon has more Data Science functionality on the way.

"Specialists in Data Science say the company has become increasingly interested in the business models of firms that make and sell pattern-finding algorithms for extremely large data sets," writes Quentin Hardy. "They theorize that Amazon wants to move beyond its Cloud services businesses – which rents data storage and raw computing power – and add to these offerings analysis software that can be rented, and possibly modified, to suit a company's needs."

"Amazon has the expertise and the computing power to do something like this," says Kyle McNabb, a vice president at research firm Forrester. "They could rent an analytics engine to people on a quarterly basis, possibly offer to match your data to other large data sets and find something useful."

Hardy: "It would not be difficult for Amazon to offer such a service, since many of the company's major products are already on Amazon Web Services, and other legacy applications are being moved there. That means that data management tools like *MapReduce* (currently a feature in Amazon Web Services), payment security and fraud detection software, and Amazon's product recommendation engine could all be in the system. While prices are dropping for the predictive and analytic software offered by the likes of SAS and EMC, the products are generally considered somewhat expensive. Amazon could remove the higher-value proprietary features from its software and sell a cheap simplified version, in the way Google created its *Google Analytics* ... service in order to increase the attractiveness of its advertising-based business."

Hardy notes that AWS has so far concentrated mostly on offering the raw materials of storage and computing to engineering teams, the so-called "back end" of computing. A move to typically higher-value "front end" products for people in areas like finance or marketing is likely, both for Amazon and others in the Cloud Computing business. Amazon has already gone from selling books to offering services whereby authors can publish their works directly on e-readers, operating Web sites for other companies, and purchased outfits like the Zappos shoe retailer to sell a broader array of goods.

Forrester's McNabb says that given the large amounts of data, and the few people qualified to make sense of it, "*someone* will offer this as a service. ... Oracle has the assets to do it, but I'm not sure they are interested. I.B.M. has the assets, and Apple could if they wanted to, with their understanding of customer behavior. Amazon is a very good candidate to make it work."

The most recent addition to Amazon's bag of Big Data tricks is is *Redshift*. This product, announced November 2012, constitutes an attractive, low-cost hosted data warehouse alternative for enterprises. *Redshift*, says Andy Jassy, AWS Senior Vice President, costs about a tenth of the price of of a traditional data warehouse. The service – scheduled for release in early 2013 – fully "automates ... deployment and administration and works with popular business intelligence tools."

This latter mentioned comparability extends to BI packages from SAP, IBM, Jaspersoft and Microstrategy, which take advantage of streamlined integration via PostgreSQL drivers combined with Open Database Connectivity (ODBC) and Java Database Connectivity (JDBC) APIs. Data – up to 1.6 petabytes stored in up to 100 2-terabyte nodes or 16-terabyte nodes – are to be stored in columnar format thus, according to Jassy, making queries run "much faster."

Databases on AWS

AWS offers powerful database options which include RDS (*Relational Database Services*), A*mazon EC2 Relational Databases AMIs*, and *Amazon SimpleDB*.

For database implementations requiring relational storage and built on MySQL or Oracle, RDS automates common administrative tasks, offers feature rich functionality that enhances database availability and scalability, significantly reducing the complexity of managing and the cost of owning database assets.

Amazon RDS automatically backs up databases and maintains your database software, allowing you to spend more time on application development. Using the Multi-AZ deployment option (currently available for MySQL only), you can have Amazon RDS provision and maintain a synchronous "standby" replica of your database in a different Availability Zone, enhancing your database availability. Additionally, the Read Replica feature available for MySQL, enables you to exploit MySQL native replication and setup replicas in minutes for read scaling. Amazon RDS for MySQL manages the replication and replicas for you. Additionally, you also benefit from the flexibility of being able to scale the compute resources or storage capacity associated with your relational database instance via few clicks or a single API call.

Amazon EC2 Relational Database AMIs allow you to use a number of leading relational databases on Amazon EC2. An Amazon EC2 instance can be used to run a database, and the data can be stored within an Amazon EBS volume. Amazon EBS is a fast and reliable persistent storage feature of Amazon EC2. *With Amazon EC2 Relational Database AMIs*, developers avoid the friction of infrastructure provisioning while gaining access to a variety of standard database engines. *Amazon EC2 Relational Database AMIs* enable developers to skip the infrastructure and hardware provisioning typically associated with installing a new database server, while still enabling them to exert complete control over the administrative and tuning tasks associated with running a database server.

Enterprises can use *Amazon EC2 Relational Database AMIs* to deploy database products from IBM and Oracle, as well as MySQL, Microsoft SQL Server, PostGre SQL, Sybase, and Enterprise DB.

Finally, for database implementations not requiring a relational model, those that only demand index and query capabilities, *Amazon SimpleDB* eliminates the administrative overhead of running a highly-available production database, and is freed from strict requirements of a RDBMS.

Amazon *SimpleDB* allows enterprises to store and query data items via simple web requests. In addition to handling infrastructure provisioning along with software installation and maintenance, *SimpleDB* indexes data, creates geo-redundant replicas of the data to guarantee secure availability, and automatically tunes customers' databases.

When dealing with workloads involving large data sets and/or demanding throughput requirements, *SimpleDB* allows enterprises to spread data sets and requests across additional machine resources via the creation of additional domains.

Finally, *SimpleDB* does not impose a rigid schema for data. The benefit for the customer is flexibility. When the nature of an enterprise's business changes, the enterprise can painlessly adapt its database to those changes without complex schema updates or costly revisions of the database code.

Windows PowerShell for AWS

Late in 2012, AWS launched *PowerShell* – a Windows interface for managing AWS services. *AWS Tools for Windows PowerShell* delivers more than 500 "cmdlets" (small, "lightweight" commands) which enable administrators to create scripts and make service calls using an intuitive, command-line-oriented environment. PowerShell enables the management of twenty key Amazon services, including S3 and EC2. With PowerShell, administrators can also run Windows Server 2012 on EC2 and liscense/install a range of Windows-compatible apps.

AWS Outages

Major outages have not been unknown with regard to AWS. The most recent as of this writing occurred in October of 2012, taking down Reddit, Foursquare, Coursera, Netflix, Pinterest and other major AWS-hosted commerce presences. The interruption lasted approximately 6 hours, inconveniencing millions of customers and costing the firms involved significant revenue. Outages are not, however, unknown to other Cloud providers either – nor to isolated, fire-walled enterprise servers off the Cloud grid. As in all other aspects of life and commerce, the occasional failure is not only an option, but an inevitability. Such is our world. With AWS, as with other Cloud providers, redundancy protects data and system breaks are addressed speedily.

IBM Cloud Services

Including IBM Platform Symphony for Breakthrough Hadoop Results and Optimal MapR Implementation

Having been one of the first in the Cloud Computing arena with its "Blue Cloud" initiative of 2007, IBM offers clients a host of enterprise class Cloud Computing capabilities. IBM brings a range of expertise and tools to the table with which managers can assess their enterprise's "Cloud readiness" and develop Return on Investment (ROI) and migration strategies. IBM provides many tools to help IT staff maximize application development time, as well as testing, by enabling these within the *IBM Smart Business Development and Test Cloud*. IBM also provides anytime, anywhere access to applications, information and resources via the *IBM Smart Desktop Cloud* ... and accelerates and simplifies deployment of a complete Cloud environment via the *IBM Cloud Service Provider Platform* (CSP2).

Additional IBM tools include elegant, powerful and robust social networking services and on-line collaboration with *IBM LotusLive Collaboration Suite*. There's also a Cloud-based platform for fast, flexible deployment of management solutions via *IBM Tivoli Live* ... turnkey solutions for high-security management of key data through the "managed backup Cloud" offered by *IBM Information Protection Services* ... and WebSphere Cast Iron Cloud Integration enabling seamless, intuitive rapid app integration.

Former IBM CEO Sam Palmisano has said he expects IBM to generate around $7 billion from Cloud Computing by 2015. Palmisano notes that IBM is already involved in "thousands" of Cloud engagements with customers such as AT&T.

IBM announced in March of 2011 that it had invested $38 million to build a new Pacific Cloud Computing Data Centre in Singapore. The announcement came a couple months after IBM said it would collaborate with China-based Range Technology Development to build the largest Cloud Computing data center in Asia, located in China's Hebei province. The new facility extends the global reach of IBM's Cloud delivery network with centers in central Germany, Canada and the United States. The company also maintains 13 global Cloud labs, of which seven are based in the Asian Pacific, including China, India, Korea, Japan, Hong Kong and Vietnam. "IBM's investment in our Asia Pacific Cloud Computing Data Centre in Singapore reflects the increase in demand for Cloud solutions and services by our clients in the region," says Paul Moung, VP of Cloud Computing at IBM Growth Markets. "The Centre will provide the highest security standards and capabilities to minimize capital expenditure and reduce operational costs."

Recently, the firm launched a new program that will do much to quicken its virtual machines (VMs). IBM's advanced virtual deployment software allows IBM to get VMs provisioned and up-and-running in a manner of seconds. Thus, in the words of Dennis Quan – Vice President of the *SmartCloud* Infrastructure at IBM and former director of IBM's Tivoli China Development Labs, client firms will be able to confidently "relinquish ... resources when they're not using them" as they know it will not take long to get them back again. "Even when you up the number of VMs you're provisioning, you still get the time benefits."

The software enables organizations to build a Cloud environment rapidly and manage it with far greater ease than previously possible. The software enables robust dynamic provisioning and scheduling of server resources. While traditional technologies deploy VMs slowly, requiring significant hands-on management from IT staff, the IBM software can deploy a single VM in seconds, dozens in a few minutes and hundreds or thousands within an hour.

In addition to speed, the new IBM software provides a powerful image management system to help organizations install, configure and automate the creation of new VMs.

Virtual server images are typically between five to 20 gigabytes in size. Multiply this number by the thousands of virtual images created today, with larger enterprises having five to twenty thousand virtual machines, and the resulting complexity makes it quite a task for IT managers tasked with maximizing service levels. This task demands an environment delivering rapid access to IT resources.

"These new technologies deliver a definitive step forward in simplifying the way IT staff can manage the Cloud," says Ric Telford, vice president of IBM Cloud Services. "They come at a critical time for businesses as the demand for computing resources and new services are becoming nearly insatiable, despite generally stagnate budgets. IBM is delivering again on our promise of leading Cloud innovation with a focus on fundamentally transforming the economics of IT."

At the same time, IBM has expanded the capabilities of its *Tivoli Provisioning Manager*, which automates best practices for data center provisioning and thereby helps organizations better manage virtual computing resources.

Another powerful tool is IBM's *Tivoli Storage Manager for Virtual Environments*. This tool simplifies the servicing of backup and recovery needs, enables online database and app protection, and eases disaster recovery, space management, archiving and retrieval. In the virtualized environment, *Tivoli Storage Manager for Virtual Environments* improves the frequency of backups to reduce the degree of data risk, and facilitates faster recovery of data to reduce downtime post-failure. By off-loading backup and restore processes from virtual machines, *Tivoli Storage Manager for Virtual Environments* allows to remain active without interruption.

January 2012 Acquisition of Green Hat

On January 4, 2012, IBM announced an agreement to acquire Green Hat, a leader in Cloud software quality and testing solutions.

Green Hat tools empower IT engineers to improve the software quality by enabling them to use Cloud Computing technologies to test applications *before* delivery. When combined with IBM's Rational Software solutions, developers and testers can achieve extremely high levels of efficiency, effectiveness and collaboration.

"The acquisition of Green Hat helps IBM customers transform software quality and agility enabled by the Cloud," says Kristof Kloeckner, General Manager, IBM Rational Software. "Green Hat's virtualization testing technology addresses the entire development lifecycle and helps accelerate the delivery of business critical software at a lower cost to the business."

Green Hat tools allow developers to test diverse software, hardware and third-party services in a wholly virtualized environment. Given this, developers can perform continuous end-to-end integration testing on applications throughout the development cycle.

"IBM's purchase of Green Hat shows where IT might get the next big wave of cost savings from virtualization," writes *InformationWeek's* Charles Babcock. "The first wave came from server virtualization, letting IT buy less hardware. The next could come from virtualizing processes – such as using virtualization to make it much cheaper to develop and test new software."

Babcock continues: "Green Hat produces a complex, virtualized environment capable of mimicking many pieces of enterprise software. Its *Virtual Integrated Environment* (VIE) can mimic 70 frequently used enterprise technologies. To new software, VIE can look like a long list of SAP or Oracle applications; it can look like Oracle's Java middleware or various messaging systems, such as Tibco's Rendevous, Software AG's WebMethods, Progress Software's Sonic MQ, or IBM's WebSphere MQ. When combined with Green Hat test management software, VIE can offer a full testing lab that can check the ability of a new application to work with other parts of the enterprise infrastructure."

IBM Platform Symphony for Big Data Analytics

IBM Platform Symphony provides developers with vital enterprise tools with which to manage distributed applications for scalable, shared-grid Big Data analytics. *Symphony* enables dozens of fast-running parallel applications for maximum speed in gathering results and optimal deployment of resources. The Advanced Edition of *Symphony* incorporates an Apache Hadoop-compatible MapReduce implementation which has been carefully and elegantly engineered for optimized low-latency, utmost reliability and resource-sharing. Of particular value,

Symphony's MapReduce implementation has been specifically engineered to automatically re-start failed services – an advantage lacking in the open-source solution.

Platform Symphony is customized for API-driven, programmatic workloads. While batch schedulers commonly schedule jobs in seconds or, at worst, minutes, *Symphony* accomplishes the same task in milliseconds. Thus it supports real-time requirements. The product's APIs are very well documented, making easy the integration of apps written in C, C++, C#, NET, Visual Basic, Java, Excel COM, R and a large number of scripting languages. Additionally, *Platform Symphony* clients and services are compatible with the full range of frameworks and operating environments. And nodes within a cluster can run multiple operating systems.

IBM Cloud Docs

In December 2012 IBM launched *Cloud Docs*, a suite of Web apps that enable the creation, editing, and sharing of presentations, documents and spreadsheets. *Cloud Docs* comes free with a subscription to *IBM's SmartCloud Engage Advanced* service for business collaboration. Otherwise it is available for a small monthly fee, per user, per month (at this writing, $3 per user per month) for orgs subscribing to *SmartCloud Engage Standard*.

"As the mobile workforce moves beyond gaining access to email and calendars to collaborate and generate new ideas and be more efficient anytime, anywhere, on any device, the intersection of social, mobile, and cloud becomes even more critical," says Alistair Rennie, IBM's general manager for social business.

The direct competitors to this product are *Microsoft Office 365* and *Google Apps for Business*, both discussed in subsequent chapters.

The utility model of computing – computing resources delivered over the network in much the same way that electricity or telephone service reaches our homes and offices – makes more sense than ever.

– Scott McNealy,Co-Founder, Sun Microsystems

Microsoft and the Cloud

Including HDInsight for Big Data

Given the marketing model on which its success to-date has been based, the entry of Microsoft into the Cloud Computing arena might seem surprising at first, save for the fact that such change is essential to Microsoft's long-term survival. For decades, Microsoft's business model has been based on the sale of one-time, flat-fee software licenses wherein users pay a set amount for the right to use a Microsoft app as much or as little as they choose.

But as Klaus Holse Andersen, Microsoft corporate vice president, told Nick Clayton of the *Wall Street Journal*: "We see it is inevitable that the Cloud is the way the world is going to go. In that case, you just have to live with the change in your business model. If you try to stick to the old business model then you become extinct at some point. I think we're really in a unique position where you can decide whether you want to be in our Cloud or a hoster's Cloud or your own private Cloud."

Microsoft Business Productivity Online Suite: SaaS

Microsoft's "Online" division – MS Online – develops and sells Microsoft-hosted software offerings like the *Business Productivity Online Suite* (BPOS) and *Dynamics CRM Online*, for on-demand customer relations management.

Aimed at servicing small businesses, Microsoft BPOS comprises a strong set of messaging and collaboration tools, delivered as a subscription service, that give clients robust capabilities without the need to deploy and maintain on-premises software and hardware.

The suite includes *Microsoft Exchange Online* for email and calendaring; *Microsoft SharePoint Online* for portals and document sharing; *Microsoft Office Communications Online* for presence availability, instant messaging, and peer to peer audio calls; and Office Live Meeting for web and video conferencing.

Microsoft also offers the security-enhanced "BPOS-Federal" for U.S. government contractors.

Note that each menu item in the BPOS suite of services is also available *ala carte*.

Via *Dynamics CRM Online*, MS Online competes with players like Oracle and Salesforce.com to provide Cloud SaaS for small and medium enterprises (SMEs) wishing to keep track of customers and their buying trends.

"What differentiates *Dynamics CRM* from the rest of the market is its usability," says Kirill Tatarinov, corporate vice-president of Microsoft Business Solutions. *"Dynamics CRM* is built inside Microsoft's *Office Outlook,* which is the most popular email platform. Customers who already use *Outlook* have an easy way to access information about their clients, pipelines, opportunities and leads from the same environment. They don't have to leave their familiar interface; they can do everything on Outlook and that's a very important and significant differentiator."

Dynamics CRM started in its original incarnation as a licensed, on-premises product for enterprises.

"CRM was a product we built from scratch but built as an on-premise product," said Microsoft Technical Fellow Mike Ehrenberg in conversation with reporter Arik Hesseldahl. "Now we're at the point where we shipped [*Dynamics CRM*] online first. We have parity between everything we can do in the Cloud and on premise, including the full aspects of customization. We've also transformed our cadence. We're off the old three-year delivery cycle. We're refreshing that service pretty much every six to nine months. But we're also maintaining the on-premise product and syncing innovation in the online environment into the on-premise one. Choice is something that no one else has. We have the same experience whether its on-premise or in the Cloud or hosted by a partner."

Thus, as you might assume, *Dynamics CRM* is a popular option for enterprises involved in, or contemplating, a hybrid Cloud approach for their customer relations data. "We see a lot of places where people have deployed CRM on-premise," says Ehrenberg, "and we've now opened up a lot of capabilities for them to customize and extend out of the *Azure* Cloud. Let's say they want to put up a custom portal that puts a different face on the data and functionality; they can build that using tools that we give them and run it in *Azure*." [Please see below for an explanation of *Windows Azure*.] "The hybrid is going to be the way of the world for everyone for a long period of time. So the ability to extend an on-premise application via the Cloud is something we're really focused on right now. Also the same thing is true with CRM online. You can develop a large custom application on *Azure*. We think the hybrid capability and the ability to have *Azure* with its elasticity, is a tremendous advantage for these things."

Windows Azure: PaaS ... with Persistant Images and Linux Support

Launched in 2010, *Windows Azure* comprises a platform Cloud within which enterprises can create and host Web apps and services that quickly scale up or down, and do so using skill sets and tools that already exist in-house.

As Microsoft's Dan'l Lewin has told journalist Matt Rosoff : "Our positioning point and value prop with Azure is that of a platform as a service [PaaS]. And we're almost exactly a year into having commercial availability of the product. ... Some of our high-profile or early adopters include this company out of France called Lokad doing some really interesting high-end math calculations in our Cloud in support of supply-chain optimization for the likes of Carrefour and Wal-Mart, things like that. The natural attraction point for *Azure* right now tends to be higher level use cases where the platform value is really clear, as opposed to the 'let's go quick and dirty off the shelf and get some storage and compute cycles and we'll be our own sysadmin.' Amazon has done incredible work and they continue to grow their infrastructure with platform-like capabilities, but most of the startups that go with Amazon, they're just quickly deploying Web servers and storage capability. And they're still doing their own administration."

According to Microsoft's own official description: "*Windows Azure* provides developers with on-demand compute and storage to host, scale, and manage web applications on the Internet through Microsoft datacenters. *Windows Azure* is a flexible platform that supports multiple languages and integrates with your existing on-premises environment. To build applications and services on *Windows Azure*, developers can use their existing *Microsoft Visual Studio* expertise. In addition, *Windows Azure* supports popular standards, protocols and languages including SOAP, REST, XML, Java, PHP and Ruby."

One key offering within *Azure* is *Microsoft SQL Azure* which customers may use to extend an existing on-premises *Microsoft SQL Server* infrastructure or as a complete off-premises database solution. Enterprises can use this product to: integrate with *SQL Server* and *Microsoft Visual Studio*, consolidate multiple data sources in the Cloud, enable secure data access from any device anywhere, innovate with scalable custom web applications, and create line-of-business and departmental applications.

"It's almost impossible to believe now, but when Microsoft premiered its *Windows Azure* service back in October 2008, there was genuine speculation over whether the company would try to muscle its way into the Cloud the way it did with Internet Explorer during the war with Netscape," writes *ReadWrite Cloud's* Scott M. Fulton III. "What was the hook? What Windows service or feature would be so irresistible that would require Azure, that no other competitor would be able to gain a footing?"

Fulton continues: "Most conspiracy theories seem stupid three years or so later, after they've failed to come to fruition. Now that Amazon is the leader (albeit amid good competition) in Cloud-based virtual machines, VMware is the leader in virtualization services for the enterprise (with Citrix keeping it on its toes), Salesforce (it's still amazing to say it) has become the leader in Cloud-based applications, and Heroku (a Salesforce product) is believed to be within striking distance of leadership in Cloud-based apps platforms, it becomes not only feasible but practical to consider *Azure* in terms of *relevance*."

Fulton sees potential relevance in persistent *images*, which Microsoft also refers to as *VM roles*. "It's the type of service that Amazon EC2, Rackspace, and GoGrid customers typically expect: deploying a server image to the public Cloud that can then be used to host an application full-time. It's not rocket science, or at least it shouldn't be."

"A VM role gives you a high degree of control over the virtual machine," reads MSDN's documentation, "while also providing the advantages of running within the *Windows Azure* environment: immediate scalability, in-place upgrades with no service downtime, integration with other components of your service, and load-balanced traffic. The VM role consists of an operating system that is constructed using a base virtual hard drive (VHD) and optionally one or more differencing VHDs. The use of the VM role also involves a service definition file and a service configuration file." Fulton: "Rather than develop and run code to be managed by a .NET Framework running in the Cloud, as *Azure's* principal PaaS service works now, users would deploy an operating system image and manage that image directly ... the way Amazon users have been doing for years. My friend Mary Jo Foley has kept her unblinking eye (I can't do that myself without it burning) on the fact that MSDN documentation refers to 'an operating system image' in a curiously agnostic fashion, as opposed to stating 'a Windows Server image' or something else equally specific. This leads Foley to believe that the company is willing to open up *Azure* to host other types of server images ... "

Indeed, Microsoft enabled Linux on its *Windows Azure Cloud* in 2012.

Microsoft SQL Server 2012

This latest edition of *SQL Server* incorporates versatile and powerful tools for easily designing, testing and deploying SQL databases and apps. Use *SQL Server* resources to manipulate and query complex data, integrate non-relational features such as geospatial data types and native file streaming, move your enterprise's database implementation to the Cloud with *Azure SQL Database*, and even create Windows Phone Cloud apps with *SQL Data Sync*.

Microsoft's BizSpark Program: An Economical Solution for Start-Ups

Microsoft's *BizSpark* program allows start-ups to access the firm's Cloud services at a premium price. Per Lewin: "We make the offer in 110 countries plus. It's a three-year use right for all of our tools and server technologies as well as a certain amount of Azure cycles and storage units. The companies entering the program need to be less than three years old when they enter and have less than $1 million in revenue [and be privately held]. Those are the three criteria."

Windows Server and Hyper-V 2012 for the Private Cloud

Microsoft's *Windows Server Hyper-V 2012 Cloud* technology allows the core of an enterprise's infrastructure and apps to be delivered in robust new ways. This private Cloud technology allows fast scaling, provisioning, automation and agility. *Hyper-V* delivers strong tools to maximize the cost savings of virtualization through *Windows Server 2012*. Via this technology, organizations can maximize server hardware investments by consolidating multiple server roles as separate virtual machines running on a single physical machine. They can also run multiple operating systems in parallel on a single server, thus fully leveraging the power of x64 computing.

Beginning with *Windows Server 2008*, server virtualization using *Hyper-V* technology has been an integral part of the operating system. *Windows Server 2008 R2* introduced a new version of *Hyper-V*, which remains incorporated with *Windows Server 2012* in its latest iteration.

Hyper-V in Windows Server 2012 delivers increased availability for virtualized data centers, improved management of same, increased performance and hardware support for *Hyper-V* VMs, excellent virtual networking performance, and a simplified method for physical and virtual computer deployments via .vhd files.

Microsoft Office 365

This cloud-based variant of Microsoft's popular Office suite incorporates *Word, Excel* and *PowerPoint*, along with a number of tools Microsoft gained with its acquisitions of Yammer and Skype. As of this writing, the price per user starts at $4 per month for the Standard Edition, and up to $20 per month for an expanded enterprise edition incorporating e-mail archiving, hosted voice-mail support and other enhancements.

HDInsight for Big Data

Announced October 2012, Microsoft's latest *Azure* enhancement is its Hadoop-compatible *HDInsight* PaaS offering, which enables rapid querying of SQL databases as well as semi-structured and unstructured data sources. The product includes a Hive ODBC driver for *Excel, Microsoft SQL Connector for Hadoop*, and *SQL Database* – a complete, fully relational database-as-a-service.

HDInsight works seamlessly with Apache Hadoop by distributing enterprise-level, Hadoop solutions over both Windows Azure and Windows Server. HD Insight is also fully compatible with such tools as Powerview, PowerPivot, and SQL Server Analysis and Reporting Services.

"The value of the service, of the *HDInsight* service, is simpler to the value proposition than you get for products." So says Microsoft's Doug Leland. "As a company, I'm not investing in the capital of the infrastructure to build out the software, and I don't have to buy a bunch of machines to build up a cluster. I don't need to hire a Hadoop expert to know how to deploy and build out a Hadoop cluster because I can go to the service, and with basically three clicks and ten minutes, I can deploy a cluster of any size. I pay for that by capacity, but again I don't need that implementation expertise. What I do need is the individual who knows how to build my jobs."

I don't know if we are always going to be talking about the Cloud; that's a word that might last three years, five years, ten years; then it's said the gift will keep on giving.

- Steve Ballmer, Microsoft CEO

Google and the Cloud

Including Google BigQuery for Gaining Real-Time Big Data Insights, Google Compute Engine for Quickly Crunching Big Data, and Google SQL

Google App Engine

A survey conducted and compiled by Bitcurrent, an analyst firm focused on emerging technologies, has ranked Google *App Engine* as the second leading Cloud offering behind Amazon Web Services. As a Google spokesperson has recently noted: "Every week, more than 150,000 applications, including many developed by start-ups such as Simperium (developer of *Simplenote*), Gri.pe, Farmigo, and others, are active on Google *App Engine*. These applications have been developed by the more than 100,000 developers at companies large and small who are working on apps powered by Google *App Engine*. Everyday, the Google *App Engine* platform powers more than one billion pageviews across all *App Engine* applications."

As a PaaS Cloud offering, the Google *App Engine* competes directly not only with AWS but also *Microsoft*

Azure. And there is nothing subtle about this rivalry. Speaking at the annual Cloud Connect conference, Microsoft developer and platform general manager Matt Thompson claimed that interest in Google's *App Engine* is "almost nonexistent" in start-ups across the country.

Despite this carping, the Google *App Engine* seems to be giving Azure a run for the money. Google *App Engine* enables IT professionals to build and host web apps on the same systems that power Google applications. Like other competitive Cloud products, *App Engine* offers rapid development and deployment; and easy and intuitive administration with no need to worry about hardware, patches or backups; also instantaneous scalability. Features include customized administration consoles empowering clients to manage all apps in their domain; a 99.9% uptime SLA, with excellent developer support always available; and extra-strong security tools.

Clients can share their apps with the world-at-large, or limit access to enterprise members.

Google *App Engine* supports apps written in several programming languages. Developers can use *App Engine's* Java runtime environment to build apps using JVM, Java servlets and the Java programming language – or any other language using a JVM-based interpreter or compiler (JavaScript, Ruby, etc.). *App Engine* as well provides a dedicated Python runtime environment incorporating a fast Python interpreter as well as the Python standard library. *App Engine* also offers a Go runtime environment running natively compiled Go code.

To get started on *App Engine* costs nothing. The system allows you to use up to 1 GB of storage, as well as adequate CPU/bandwidth to efficiently run an app serving approx. 5 million page-views per month, without charge. As your usage grows, and you enable billing, you are only charged for resources used above the previous free level.

App Engine for Business

Having debuted in 2011, *App Engine* for Business delivers all the efficiencies of *App Engine*, but with additional tools to manage enterprise use cases, and more robust APIs for business-critical applications. Most importantly, *App Engine* for Business includes a number of premium services. These include SQL (providing access to the full capabilities of a dedicated relational database, without having to have to *manage* the damn thing) and also SSL (Secure Sockets Layer) for your domain-specific apps.

Google Apps

Google Apps is a convenient SaaS Cloud service providing access to g-mail and *Google Calendar, Google Docs* and *Google Sites*, and *Google Reader, Blogger, Picasa Web Albums* and *AdWords*.

Up until early December of 2012, *Google Apps* were available free, but going forward will be a pay-service. At this writing, $50 per year per user.

Google Docs provides very good tools for the creation, editing and distribution of documents, spreadsheets and presentations accessible from any device (even smartphones). *Google Docs* works via browser on Windows, Mac, and Linux, and supports the standard popular formats: .doc, .xls, .ppt, and .pdf. Of course, all files are backed-up online and readily accessible. Administrators have tools to manage permissions system-wide; and individual document owners can grant or revoke access whenever they want.

Google Sites delivers robust and efficient tools with which to create secure web pages for intranets and team projects – with no coding or HTML required. *Google Sites* is especially useful for organizing vital information securely while at the same time centralizing documents, spreadsheets, presentations, videos, slideshows and more in one easily accessed and navigated ecosystem. The app includes templates for building project workspaces, team sites, etc. Like *Google Docs*, *Google Sites* is securely powered by the web, allowing users to access their company pages at any time from anywhere. Like *Google Docs*, the app works across Windows, Mac and Linux machines on the web. And as with *Google Docs*, administrators and authors possess rigorous permissions controls.

Google Apps for Business

Available at a slightly higher fee, *Google Apps for Business* includes everything offered by plain-vanilla *Google Apps*, but also delivers Google Video and Google Groups for Business ... 25GB email storage per user, with BlackBerry and Microsoft Outlook interoperability ... SSO, forced SSL, and custom password strength requirements ... a 99.9% uptime guarantee ... plus 24/7 support.

Through *Google Video for Business*, Google securely hosts and streams an enterprise's videos. Thus users don't need to share over email, or force IT to develop and manage an enterprise-specific video solution. *Google Video* enables organizations to securely share at anytime and from anywhere on any device.

Via *Google Groups for Business*, client organizations can easily and seamlessly share calendars, folders, docs, and sites. Designated administrators oversee group membership by manipulating customizable subscription settings. Group discussions can be archived and are easily searchable by allowed users via the web.

Google Cloud Connect

With the launch of *Google Cloud Connect* in February of 2011, Google took direct aim at converting and claiming Microsoft's large applications user-base. The app comprises an easy and inviting bridge for enterprises wishing to migrate from Microsoft products to *Google Docs* and other Google tools in the Cloud.

Per Google's own product documentation, *Google Cloud Connect* is designed to allow Cloud collaboration (such as multi-person, simultaneous editing) for those *"Microsoft Word, Excel* and *PowerPoint* applications that coworkers *may still need from time to time.* More people will be able to achieve a 100% web future entirely in *Google Docs* after learning the benefits of web-powered collaboration within traditional software. ... For example, you can edit a *Word* document's table of contents from Dublin while coworkers adjust formatting and make revisions from Denver. Instead of bombarding each other with attachments and hassling to reconcile people's edits, your whole team can focus on productive work together. ... *Google Cloud* Connect *vastly improves Microsoft Office,* so companies can start using web-enabled teamwork tools *without upgrading Microsoft Office or implementing SharePoint* ... " (Italics are mine. - Lars Nielsen.)

Critics have noted only one major flaw in *Google Cloud Connect*: complete lack of Macintosh support. This is not, however, the fault of Google's engineers. Such compatibility is nigh impossible to achieve given the lack of support for open APIs on *Microsoft Office for Mac.*

Google Cloud Print

Via *Google Cloud Print*, enterprises can easily make remote printers available to users. Google Cloud Print functions well on phones, tablets, Chromebooks, and PCs.

Google's Cloud Robotics Strategy

At the 2011 Google I/O developer's conference, Google announced a new initiative called "Cloud robotics" in conjunction with robot manufacturer Willow Garage. Google has developed an open source (free) operating system for robots, with the unsurprising name "ROS" – or *Robot Operating System*. In other words, Google is trying to create the MS-DOS (or MS Windows) of robotics.

"With ROS, software developers will be able to write code in the Java programming language and control robots in a standardized way," notes software developer Martin Ford, much in the same way that programmers writing applications for Windows or the Mac can access and control computer hardware."

Google's approach also offers compatibility with Android. Robots. The robots will be able to take advantage of the "Cloud-based" (in other words, online) features used in Android phones, as well as new Cloud-based capabilities specifically for robots. In essence this means that much of the intelligence that powers the robots of the future may reside on huge server farms, rather than in the robot itself. While that may sound a little "Skynet-esque," it's a strategy that could offer huge benefits for building advanced robots.

Google Drive

A major recent tool from Google is *Google Drive*, an easy, intuitive tool that syncs files on your computer to backup versions in the Cloud. For most user-levels, the service is free. The tools are easily downloadable from Google, and simple to install on any PC. Go for it.

Google BigQuery, Compute Engine and SQL

Google BigQuery provides an excellent tool for using a RESTful API and a SQL-like query language to gain meaningful, actionable, real-time business intelligence (including nearly instantaneous trend detection) from Big Data. This streamlined platform allows enterprises to run efficient, ad hoc SQL queries in mere seconds on multi-terabyte datasets. *BigQuery* allows the storage of hundreds of terabytes of data – all of it completely secure, backed up on multiple sites and protected by easily-implemented access control lists.

Such firms as Claritics, Boo-box and redBus have used *BigQuery* to date, with good results. Raj Pei, Claritics CEO, says of the service that it offers "significant time-to-market performance advantages." Boo-box Chief Technology Officer Thyago Liberalli notes that *BigQuery* allows his firm to "provide … customers information that we couldn't in the past. This improves their engagement with the service and has … increased their ad spend." redBus Technology Architect Pradeep Kumar says *BigQuery* has "made large-scale data collection and crunching possible with little effort, which has translated to a significant business advantage."

BigQuery is enhanced by the instant availability of companion services such as *Google Compute Engine*, which enables enterprises to run massive workloads on Google-hosted Linux virtual machines, and *Google SQL*, which empowers enterprises to run mySQL databases on the Google Cloud.

Google Cloud Failures and Criticisms

No Cloud environment – including Google's – is immune to failure.

For example, Google's g-mail experienced a major outage on December 10th, 2012. The outage was blamed by Google execs on a routine update misfiring. In addition to the g-mail crash, some Chrome browsers saw failures as well. "As the distinction between native clients and cloud services blurs," writes one industry analyst, "enterprises cannot put up with this instability."

Chrome developer Tim Steele has indicated that concurrent problems with Google's Chrome Sync servers were caused by an incorrectly implemented change in the load-balancing configuration of the quota management system. This made the Sync service "throttle 'all' data types, without accounting for the fact that not all client versions support all data types. "That change was to a piece of infrastructure that many services at Google depend on. This means other services may been affected at the same time ..."

For enterprise users, the implications of this cascading scenario are quite disturbing.

Per a writer for *Unified Communications Strategies*: "Cloud services are expected to go down occasionally. But when a natively installed rich client in a user's machine crashes as well, it thwarts other tasks while it waits for the original service to restart. Usually, an enterprise IT shop extensively tests any software before it sends anything to production. Enterprise procurement and configuration are processes set back months behind the consumer market. These measures prevent the aforementioned scenario from occurring. Cloud-based technology is here to stay. The benefits of cloud computing are multifaceted and remarkable. But it is important to note the possible security issues surrounding cloud-based apps like Google and *Office 365*. If Google wants to be taken seriously as an enterprise player, it is imperative that the company test its configuration changes properly before going live."

Storm Clouds

Eric Sloane

Mid 20th-Century

Private Collection

Red Hat

Including Red Hat Enterprise Linux for Big Data, OpenShift and Other Goodies

If Red Hat were a teenager, it'd be the coolest teenager in town. If it were a band, it'd be the Grateful Dead. But what is it really? Try, the first-ever billion-dollar open source software company. By describing Red Hat as open source, we mean that Red Hat's core philosophy embraces the key assumption that our best ideas evolve from developing a simple, solid kernel of an idea, and then setting employees, customers and partners free to innovate and help make it better. Perhaps that's why Red Hat insiders refer to their firm as a "catalyst of communities."

"In an open source company the goal is not to manage plans and bodies of work in the traditional sense," wrote *Forbes* contributor Peter High in December of 2012. "Senior team members don't mandate what the organization should do. Instead, the focus is on building a strong work culture and catalyzing behavior. It does not mean that people don't have to have destinations in mind, and that the company is not focused on financial results. The company's stock is up more than three fold since the beginning of 2009. That said, providing employees the liberty to find their own path to the value they have signed up for is critical."

Key to Red Hat's success has been enterprises modernizing their data centers and preparing their infrastructures for Cloud Computing. "The comprehensive portfolio that Red Hat has developed with platform, virtualization and middleware products provides enterprise customers with a foundation to deploy the next generation infrastructure," says CEO Jim Whitehurst.

One of Red Hat's star products, the data center operating system platform called Red Hat Enterprise Linux, has emerged – in the words of one analyst – as "the OS of choice for private Cloud architectures."

"The role of IT has never been more important within the enterprise," comments Jim Totten, vice president and general manager of Red Hat's Platform Business Unit. "In a recent Gartner and *Forbes* survey of Board of Directors, the percent of respondents that rated IT's strategic business value contribution as high or extremely high doubled between 2010 and 2012. The rising expectations of executives require IT to be even more agile when addressing the needs of the business. In response, we're seeing a trend towards convergence of compute, storage and network as integrated infrastructure in the next few years. Many of our customers are also looking to standardize their infrastructure to become more efficient. Many of those that have standardized on Red Hat Enterprise Linux across virtual, physical and cloud deployments are able to manage more servers and users per administrator and experience significantly less downtime."

Totten continues: "Operating systems have always served two primary purposes: to enable software and developers to consume and take advantage of hardware innovations as they become available and to deliver a stable foundation on which applications can run. Moving forward, operating systems will continue to evolve in these ways to power the cloud. Take Linux as an example. Linux was developed on and for the Internet and has evolved to support 8 out of every 10 cloud-based applications today.[drop a footnote with the backup for this statement] This is because it's portable, secure, scalable and reliable - all while being open and standards-based. The cloud demands choice and flexibility, and we believe that's what will maintain Linux the cloud operating system well into the future, and we expect Red Hat Enterprise Linux to play a key role in that future too. Red Hat Enterprise Linux enables applications to consume compute, storage and network resources on a broad range of virtualization solutions and cloud services from many vendors, with a commitment for stability over a ten year life cycle." Furthermore, Totten sees the product as having special appeal re: Big Data operations: "An enterprise platform like Red Hat Enterprise Linux integrates high performance, scalable storage and data throughput with the ability to successfully develop, integrate and secure applications consuming data."

Late 2012 Update/Expansion for Red Hat Enterprise Virtualization (RHEV) Platform and Integration with Red Hat Storage

Version 3.1 – released December 2012 – improves Red Hat's Kernel-based Virtual Machine hypervisor so as to allow it to scale down to x86 processors, support current industry-standard x86 processors, and integrate RHEV with *Red Hat Storage*, the firm's scale-out, open-source storage solution for data management. As well, 3.1 expands the platform's ability to scale while supporting guest Vms – up to 160 logical CPUs and 2 terabytes of memory per VM.

Red Hat Storage is, of course, based on the GlusterFS technology the company acquired when it bought Gluster, Inc. in Oct. 2011. GlusterFS comprises an open-source, distributed file system built using a stackable user space design. GlusterFS "clusters" storage units using Infiniband RDMA of TCP/IP.

Whitehurst sees the firm's 2011 acquisition of Gluster as having been a key strategic move for maintaining Red Hat's current rate of growth. At the time of the acquisition, Whitehurst explained that he was excited about "further expansion of our market opportunity and footprint in the data center by entering the storage space via the acquisition of the open source software company, Gluster, Inc. This software-only solution addresses storage of unstructured data spanning from bare metal to virtualized instances and in Cloud deployments. This $4 billion addressable market, which is growing rapidly, is a great place for Red Hat to enter the Big Data world and provide storage in the Cloud. Storage is complementary to our business, fits with our core infrastructure stack and is aligned with our enterprise customer base. Also, the Gluster technology has me excited. It is a software solution for solving the scale-out storage problem. It's open source with a vibrant community and fits w ell with our Cloud vision of being able to deploy applications anywhere. It's already used by companies like Pandora and Limelight [ph] for their unstructured data needs."

Whitehurst continues: "Because the IT landscape is changing, storage architectures are changing, too. Traditional hardware-based storage solutions present a problem for customers who are now faced with having to replicate data in multiple Cloud, including on-premise and public. There's a need for a common storage solution for customer data, whether that data -- wherever that data maybe. Because Gluster is software-based, it's a great solution for the challenge of storage in the Cloud. For example, you can't ship hardware to Amazon to run on top of their Cloud but you can move the Gluster solution into a virtual machine instance running on a public Cloud. Gluster provides choice. It's already available on Amazon's Cloud, and we are driving innovation to enable it with other Cloud offerings. The Gluster technology, now known as *Red Hat Storage,* will be a foundation to bring products to market that not only provide a compelling value and performance proposition but solve some of the new challenges of storing the explosion of unstructured data."

CloudForms, Red Hat Cloud Virtualization Bundle, Red Hat Hybrid IaaS Solution, and the Open IaaS Architecture Service

Late in 2012, Red Hat announced version 1.1 of its popular *CloudForms* management software and also made available three additional Cloud offerings created to help businesses initiate Cloud Computing.

CloudForms provides self-service system management for operating systems and apps running jointly together in the Cloud or within a company's own infrastructure. *CloudForms* is meant to eventually supplant the firm's well-known Red Hat Network Satellite administrations package. *CloudForms* 1.1 delivers easy tools for such tasks as deploying operating system security updates on a range of systems. Red Hat has also extended the software's LDAP support and integrated a feature that allows administrators to search their systems for specific content.

Additional new Cloud offerings include:

- *Red Hat Cloud with Virtualization Bundle* – this combining *CloudForms* with *Red Hat Enterprise Virtualization* (RHEV).

- *Red Hat Hybrid IaaS Solution* – providing tools for the creation and management of Hybrid Clouds. The package includes CloudForms and RHEV, along with Red Hat Enterprise Linux (RHEL), serving as a guest operating system.

- And *Open IaaS Architecture Service* – this allowing the installation of CloudForms and RHEV within an enterprise's proprietary IT infrastructure to enable a private IaaS Cloud.

Cloud OpenStack

Red Hat has recently (November 2012) updated its *Cloud OpenStack* platform distribution from the Essex Release to the Folsom Release. Folsom was issued by the upstream OpenStack community in September 2012. The release includes substantial new block storage and cloud-networking tools. Of course, OpenStack is a multi-stakeholder cloud platform project with participation from many tech industry leaders. Andy Cathrow, Senior Product Marketing Manager at Red Hat, emphasizes that the Red Hat version is just a preview release. He points out that the *Red Hat Cloud OpenStack* platform is as not yet a full Red Hat-supported product, and that there remains much work to be done to incorporate necessary stability and appropriate enterprise hardening. "This is [just] upstream Folsom with some bug fixes and packaging," says Cathrow.

Red Hat Cloud Foundations

The *Red Hat Cloud Foundations* family of products incorporates virtualization, Cloud management, operating system, middleware, and application management, as well as scheduling tools, software cookbooks and reference architectures packaged with step-by-step instructions, consulting, and training.

Enterprises may use *Red Hat Cloud Foundations* tools to build private Clouds utilizing RHEV or VMware ESX Server. Foundations tools may also be used to run and manage applications inside the datacenter or in Red Hat Certified public Clouds, including Amazon EC2 ... and to maximize the performance of existing infrastructure through Red Hat's open source interoperable Cloud architecture.

"In our extensive research, we've found that open APIs and interoperability are essential to customers considering the Cloud," says Gary Chen, research manager, Enterprise Virtualization Software at IDC. "Our research shows that 80 percent of enterprises cite the lack of interoperability standards as a challenge in adopting Cloud Computing services. With *Cloud Foundations*, Red Hat is on the right track with Cloud by accelerating interoperability and portability to prevent Cloud lock in."

Red Hat Platform as a Service with OpenShift

Released November 2012, Red Hat's *OpenShift Enterprise* leverages cGroups and and SELinux, and is of course built upon *Red Hat Enterprise Linux*. The product can be run on bare metal or, as well, standard virtualization hypervisors such as Red Hat's *Enterprise Virtualization* or VMware. At this writing (December 2012), Red Hat engineers are busily at work on *OpenShift Enterprise* support for OpenStack.

JBoss Operations Network

Red Hat's *JBoss Operations Network* [JON] enables total management of applications and services across physical, virtual and Cloud resources. JON provides a single point of control for deploying, managing and monitoring JBoss Enterprise Middleware, applications and services across all environments.

"It's all about the recognition that continual management of a company's production environment is getting more complicated and yet is even more crucial to the business," says Alan Santos, product manager for Red Hat's JBoss unit.

Santos: "Among our core appdev audience, JBoss has been very successful, even against the big [middleware] guys like IBM, Oracle and so on. That's because we're simpler to use, and we can be counted on by that community to meet their needs. We want JON to carry on that momentum to the whole enterprise and let IT operations managers know that JBoss can meet their needs also, no matter whether they use physical, virtualization, Cloud or any combination."

Additional Red Hat Resources

Enterprises may also use *Red Hat Enterprise MRG Grid* for flexible workload scheduling and orchestration across diverse Clouds, plus real-time adaptation to capacity supply and demand.

Be nice to nerds. Chances are you'll end up working for one.

- Bill Gates

Cloud in a Box

The Pre-Fab Track to a Robust Private Cloud

A "Cloud in a Box" is a set of off-the-shelf, integrated Cloud stacks such as are available from Cisco and Hewlett-Packard. These Cloud stacks are the "prefabricated homes" of private Cloud Computing, providing prepackaged Cloud building blocks ready for launch on demand.

"We're talking about either pure software or packaged hardware and software solutions that instantiate infrastructure as a service – meaning, when you turn the system on, you immediately can do some provisioning of virtual machines, virtual disks and virtual networks," says James Staten, vice president and principal analyst with Forrester Research. At this point, Forrester recognizes only very few products as true Cloud in a box. On the hardware and software side, its short list includes HP *CloudSystem*, Dell *Virtual Integrated System* (VIS), Cisco's *Cloud Infrastructure*, IBM *CloudBurst*,. BMC *Cloud Lifecycle Management, Cloud.com CloudStack*, Microsoft *Hyper-V Cloud* and VMware *vCloud* are software-based examples.

Cloud in a Box does have its critics."Unless you nail it right, which is unlikely, don't try to use Cloud in a Box as the platform for growing your complete Cloud infrastructure. It's unlikely to meet your expectations or needs over the long term ... so while you might get some fun technology out of it, eventually it'll be stuck in the corner somewhere with lights and disks but doing nothing." So says John Treadway, global director of Cloud solutions at Unisys.

But Staten doesn't see this happening, as whatever Cloud in a Box an enterprise chooses will inevitably share underlying hardware with the existing production environment. Additionally, "the software that makes up a Cloud system will include the automation tools that a customer would already have or would likely introduce over the next couple of years anyway."

There are no rules of architecture for a castle in the clouds.

- G. K. Chesterton (1874-1936), who was many things, but by no means a technologist.

Apple and Other Purveyors of Consumer Cloud Services

Firms such as Apple, Google and Amazon have built enormous Internet service hubs created to store and ynchronize consumers' expanding digital lives in the way of content and media.

Whether calling it an "ecosystem" or "Cloud Computing," various device creators are endeavoring to stake claims in this fast-growing area. However, only a few look likely to survive, in large measure because people don't want to spread their content over a range of different platforms. And while several companies have strength in certain areas, such as a robust hardware offerings (ala Barnes & Noble's Nook), few offer the coimplete package like Apple, Google and Amazon.

"Lenovo and Acer are following software giants such as Apple, Google and Microsoft into the Cloud with services that make your music, videos, photos, and documents available instantly across all your devices, says *PC World's* Ian Paul. "Acer will introduce a new free service called AcerCloud available on all new Acer PCs starting in the spring that instantly syncs data across your PCs, smartphones, and tablets. Lenovo's 'Personal Cloud' vision, meanwhile, will also sync data across PCs, the newly announced Lenovo S2 smartphone, and tablets, as well as the company's newly announced Android 4.0-based K91 Smart TV."

Paul: "Acer is taking a cue from Apple's iCloud with AcerCloud, a free service scheduled to become available in the spring on all new Acer PCs for syncing documents, music, photos, and videos across devices. At launch, AcerCloud will sync to Android smartphones, with Windows Phone functionality coming at a later date. Acer's plan to automatically sync data across devices. AcerCloud will include three components: PicStream to sync photos, AcerCloud docs for documents, and clear.fi Media to sync music and videos. PicStream will move any photos you take with your smartphone and save them to your main PC. Photos via PicStream will also be available on your other devices for 30 days."

Of course, Cloud-based consumer services such as these have little to do with Cloud services designed to address the IT needs of businesses, and I mention them only briefly here simply to acknowledge their existence and importance in the emerging digital retail information businesses.

VMware, Cetas, EMC, Greenplum, The Pivotal Initiative and Big Data

Owned by EMC, VMware offers an extensive solution set for building and managing public, hybrid and private Clouds, not to mention SaaS, PaaS and IaaS offerings. It also boasts an extensive partner ecosystem.

VMware's Cloud solutions are designed to dramatically simplify the provisioning and deployment of IT services while simultaneously enforcing strong control, data integrity safeguards, and regulatory compliance.

VMware products share a robust management and security model. Based on open standards, VMware's offerings are designed to liberate clients from vendor lock-in, ensuring app portability between in-house datacenters and external Clouds provided by VMware *vCloud* partners. As well, the VMware Cloud application platform allows developers to build elegant, efficient applications that are portable, dynamic, and optimized for elastic, completely scalable deployment on such public Clouds as *VMforce* and *Google App Engine*.

VMware standardizes the automation of IT services provisioning and management. Using VMware resources, customers can easily deploy preconfigured IT services from a Web-based catalog. Customers also receive customized services in real time on-demand. Thus administrators can be relieved of the bulk of maintenance tasks, while never relinquishing control of policies, regulatory compliance, etc.

VMware tools allow IT resources to be pooled and then abstracted into manageable building-blocks re: storage, network, and server units. In other words, virtual datacenters are created. These resource containers can then be dynamically allocated to the range applications, governed by customer-defined defined business rules and, of course, demand.

Recently, VMware engineers demonstrated how their integrated offerings can run a *separate instance of Android* in a virtual machine that is hosted by an Android-based smartphone.

As VMware director of product management Hoofar Razavi points out, the ability to have a separate Android instance running on a handset opens up a very wide range of possibilities. The key advantage is to those users who want to keep their handset digital personas (personal vs. work) completely separated. (BTW, the VM Android instances are completely encrypted.)

The Pivotal Initiative for Big Data

Late in 2012, VMware and its owner EMC confirmed they will merge several product divisions into a new initiative – *The Pivotal Initiative* - focused on tools for cloud computing and Big Data. The plans call for VMware to integrate that firm's Cloud Foundry PAAS, along with the 2013 spring line of tools focused on Java Developers, VMware's GemFire software for data management, and the firm's Cetas Big Data analytics division. Add to this EMC's Greenplum for Big Data, and the same firm's Pivotal Labs for a total of 600 VMware employees and 800 EMC employees combined in the new initiative.

Per a VMware spokesperson: "We are experiencing a major change in the wide scale move to cloud computing, which includes both infrastructural transformation and transformation of how applications will be built and used based on cloud, mobility, and big data. There is a significant opportunity for both VMware and EMC to provide thought and technology leadership, not only at the infrastructure level, but across the rapidly growing and fast-moving application development and big data markets. Aligning these resources is the best way for the combined companies to leverage this transformational period, and drive more quickly towards the rising opportunities."

Most Pivotal Initiative components are firms acquired in recent years by either VMware or EMC. A joint VMware/EMC announcement emphasized the critical need to remain focused on end-user benefits and computing, with emphasis given to VMware's *Virtual Desktop* as well as other products aimed at end-users (including the *Zimbra* e-mail and collaboration suite).

"*The Pivotal Initiative* will enable a new generation of workloads that can exploit the advancements VMware is driving in the datacenter," continued the announcement. "By realigning resources within *The Pivotal Initiative*, VMware can more fully focus resources on delivering the software defined datacenter, the de facto infrastructure at the heart of cloud computing, and on end-user computing–two areas where we see tremendous opportunity for growth." Of course, all products within the Initiative will be optimized with reference to the *VMware vCloud Suite*.

Solar Effect in Clouds - Ocean

Gustave Le Grey

Albumen Print from Glass Negative

Circa 1856

British Museum

Hewlett-Packard, Oracle/Sun Microsystems, Cisco Systems, Virtual Computing Environment Coalition/Acadia, Rackspace and GoGrid

Hewlett-Packard

"Cloud Computing will form the foundation of HP's future direction," writes *Computer Weekly's* Chris Saran, "but [the company] is hoping [to] encourage IT departments to continue to buy HP servers, by offering a hybrid environment. [Company leaders say] HP's hybrid approach combines the best of traditional environments with private and public Clouds, and will be the prevailing model for large enterprises for a long time. HP will continue to develop its hardware, software and services businesses."

InfoWorld's David Linthicum is not impressed. He sees HP as arriving at the Cloud party way too late. "The problem is that the IaaS, PaaS, and Big Data ships have sailed. Although few people doubt that HP can get some sort of offering to market, the chances of pulling even with the existing providers (such as IBM, Google, Amazon, and even Microsoft) are pretty slim ... AWS (Amazon Web Services) is well incorporated in the IaaS space, and PaaS is a much smaller and emerging market held soundly by Google, Microsoft, and AWS. HP, like other traditional hardware vendors, is between the proverbial rock and a hard place. Cloud Computing will ultimately erode its sales and margins on hardware and software sold to enterprises and governments. What's more, replacing this lost revenue with Cloud services will be difficult or even cannibalistic."

Pundit Kier Thomas seems equally skeptical. "Just a few years ago it was *de rigueur* for once-mighty companies to grasp at open source to plug holes in their businesses ..." he writes. "Now it feels like companies grasp at Cloud Computing instead. But in many ways the Cloud presents far more of a challenge, and requires massive innovation. And there simply isn't any evidence that HP has what it takes."

Oracle and Sun Microsystems

Oracle has taken its own sweet time in embracing the Cloud model, and has up to recently – with its acquisition of Sun Microsystems – appeared outright antagonistic to the approach. Few in the industry can forget CEO Larry Ellison's leading the charge against the Cloud with a now-famous 2008 rant about it being nothing more than a "fashion" of the moment. Two years later, Ellison adopted far milder rhetoric: "Everything's called Cloud now. If you're in the data center, it's a private Cloud. There's nothing left but Cloud Computing. People say I'm against Cloud Computing – how can I be against Cloud Computing when that's all there is?" In the course of the same remarks, Ellison put his mouth on what appears to be the linchpin of Oracle's Cloud strategy going forward: Oracle software and hardware powering the resources of other Cloud providers. Oracle seems – in the words of one industry analyst – focused on becoming "arms dealer" to Amazon and other Cloud behemoths.

Early in January 2012, Oracle demonstrated its seriousness about competing in the Big Data arena by releasing the *Oracle Big Data Appliance*. The appliance includes key software from Cloudera, the leading provider of Hadoop system management tools and support services.

Cisco Systems

In an effort to accommodate enterprise users looking to implement private and hybrid Clouds, Cisco unveiled in 2012 an "integrated" WAN routing system of existing, but enhanced, products.

Cisco's *Integrated Enterprise WAN Solution* (IEWS) is comprised of its ASR 1000 edge router, ISR branch routers and WAAS WAN optimization appliances. This is designed to "empower enterprises to connect to the Cloud via an application-aware infrastructure that is simple to manage and provision," says Praveen Akkiraju, senior vice president and general manager of Cisco's Network Services Technology Group.

"We're leveraging our extensive network footprint and credibility to connect [users] to Cloud assets," Akkiraju says.

IEWS is specifically optimized for Cloud connectivity, but the product can also facilitate traditional infrastructure deployments. The product is designed to be customizable for any enterprise user's specific needs and environment, whether a private WAN, private Cloud, or part of a hybrid Cloud solution.

Management of IEWS is through *Cisco Prime*, launched in the spring of 2011.

Cisco's share of the enterprise router market is 52% in the high end, and 84% in access routers, according to a study by the Dell'Oro Group.

Late in March 2011 Cisco Systems announced plans to buy privately held software company newScale Inc. in a deal that significantly ramped up its Cloud Computing capabilities. NewScale, which makes portals for Cloud Computing, had at the time of the acquisition more than 2 million users worldwide, including 20 percent of the *Fortune 50* companies. NewScale's customers include AT&T, American Express and Siemens.

Cisco executives have repeatedly affirmed to channel partners that they are *not* looking to make Cisco a Cloud provider. Rather, they say they want to enable channel partners to build Cloud architectures and develop Cloud services to sell to customers using Cisco gear. To help, they've introduced three Cloud designations for partners.

Cisco's *Cloud Builder Program* is customized for partners who focus on the infrastructure level of Cloud implementations. These are organizations and individuals which design, build and deploy Cloud-ready infrastructure for customers, consolidating networks, servers, storage and virtualization.

Cisco's *Cloud Provider Program* is customized for those wishing to develop and provide public Cloud services for the market.

Finally, partners participating in Cisco's *Cloud Services Reseller Program* tend to focus strictly on cooperating with *Cloud Provider* partners to resell Cloud services.

"You cannot open up a magazine, read a newspaper, watch a TV commercial without hearing the word 'Cloud,'" says Edison Peres, Cisco's senior vice president of worldwide channels. "I don't want to downplay it. It's important. It's here. I want to talk about it a little bit more, but I do want to be very clear. If all you see on the horizon is Clouds or Cloud, I want to suggest your focus is much too narrow. Cloud is part of a broad set of opportunities that we have before us.

"Choose your role in Cloud. It's here. It's real. I don't see it as a threat," Peres continues. "I see it as a clear opportunity. But you do need to choose your role. The customers' requirements are changing. They want scalable, on-demand compute and storage." He adds that customers are also looking to move from capital expenditures on IT to operational expenditures.

Peres notes that in some ways customers are better prepared for the new world of Cloud Computing than is the IT industry itself. "It's taken some time for the technology to evolve to the point that it's now able to meet customers' requirements." Peres believes the cornerstone of private Cloud infrastructure is tied into the Cisco's Virtual Computing Environment (VCE) which the company formed as a joint venture with VMware and EMC. Peres further says he expects Cloud infrastructure to grow at a compounded rate of 25 percent per year over the next few years, with 75 percent of that infrastructure growth coming from private Clouds.

Virtual Computing Environment Coalition and Acadia

In November of 2009, Cisco and EMC, together with VMware, introduced the Virtual Computing Environment Coalition. Through this joint venture, they seek to enhance the processing power of enterprises through greater IT infrastructure flexibility while at the same time lowering the total costs for IT, energy and facilities through the virtualization of pervasive data centers and transition to private Clouds.

The Virtual Computing Environment Coalition offers enterprises an accelerated approach to data center transformation. The idea is to create strong efficiencies that incorporate significant reductions in both capital investment and ongoing operating expenses. Thus, organizations will no longer be forced to choose between best-of-breed technologies and end-to-end vendor accountability.

Through *Vblock Infrastructure Packages*, the Virtual Computing Environment Coalition provides enterprises with an economical yet powerful approach to streamlining and optimizing IT strategies around private Clouds. *Vblock Infrastructure Packages* are fully integrated, tested, validated, and ready-to-go/ready-to-grow products that combining best-in-class virtualization, networking, computing, storage, security, and management tools from EMC, Cisco and VMware.

The coalition scales customer adoption of *Vblock* by enabling a world-wide community of systems integrators, channel partners, service providers and indie software vendors (ISVs). The coalition has also configured integrated pre-sale, professional services and support infrastructure to ease the process of customer engagement.

In announcing the Virtual Computing Environment Coalition, Cisco and EMC at the same time announced Acadia, a joint venture focused on easing customer build-outs of private Clouds through end-to-end integration of service providers and enterprise customers. Acadia's custom "build, operate, transfer" model for delivering the *Vblock* architecture offers maximum customers choice, flexibility and price advantages as they seek to create private Cloud installations. In addition to Cisco and EMC as the lead investors, the build-out of Acadia has also seen investment from Intel and VMware. (Note: The *Vblock* architecture relies heavily on Intel Xeon processors and other Intel data center technology for servers, storage, and networking.)

Rackspace Hosting

"In 2010, we launched the channel as a strategic piece of our business," comment Chris Rajiah Rackspace Hosting's new (as of January 2012) VP of Worldwide Channel sales. "In 2011, our key accomplishment was the unification of our disparate channel programs into one, worldwide for our over 7,000 partners – from small SMBs to large global integrators. Our onboarding process was also improved and simplified in 2011."

In 2012 Rackspace increased its presence in key areas by enhancing the range of partner programs, building improved turn-key solution sets for partners, and empowering partners to build robust models enabling them to become more of an IT-as-a-service partner.

"The enhancement partner program ... involve[s] more dedicated resources for our top tier partners," Rajiah says. "Training is a big piece of it. Partners need to clearly understand the technology layer so they can properly overlay their services. Marketing will be increased as well, with new tools, webinars, co-branded capabilities, joint event partnerships and white papers."

The latest solution sets are designed around specific key aggregation points

"We have done these aggregation points successfully, such as backup and recovery with EMC and NetApp. We want more of those horizontal alignments that have done well. Vertically, we also want to build a stronger presence in digital media, content management, collaboration and commerce."

Rackspace hopes for partners to evolve their own proprietary models to support IT-as-a-service, offering a broad choice of private, public and hybrid Cloud options.

"We also want them to apply our Fanatical Support in their OPEX models – leverage it and sell services on top of it," says Rajiah.

"Our digital media and e-commerce partners – they get it. Experienced MSPs get it. ISPs get it. Some of the traditional hardware vendors, well, our job there is to continue to provide them with Cloud thought leadership, make them comfortable understanding the technology layer, get them to understand how to deliver an on-premise experience off-premise. The part of the VAR community that isn't getting it is why we are investing in training and accreditation and programs to help them."

Early in December 2012, Rackspace announced that it would soon roll-out enhanced features and services related to its Cloud platform. Seven new services include robust tools for capacity planning, scaling architecture, patching, configuration, security guidance, monitoring, and database tuning/optimization. Rackspace's *Open Cloud Platform* is meant to offer an optimized Cloud experience for all customers.

GoGrid: Public IaaS Cloud Benefits on Dedicated Servers

GoGrid is an IaaS provider. Configuring and managing infrastructure within the GoGrid Cloud is not unlike managing infrastructure in a proprietary enterprise data center or via a dedicated server or colocation service provider. The GoGrid infrastructure is accessed via standard network protocols and IP addresses. Go Grid offers a range of Cloud hosting options, including a number of inexpensive options for small businesses.

Programmer - an organism that turns coffee into software.

- Unknown

Cloud Security, the Need for Data Loss Prevention (DLP), And Various Other Fun Stuff

Writing in *Forbes*, Microsoft's Rik Fairlie has said CIOs must make sure the Cloud Computing solution they opt for meets all their key security needs. If developing either a public Cloud or hybrid Cloud presence, "CIOs should nail down service level agreements for security and ensure the Cloud provider understands the key performance indicators needed to manage risks and performance. ... Issues to consider include data encryption, data storage location, user access, and incident response."

Before public Cloud Computing can finally become the *de facto* IT delivery and consumption standard, the onus is on vendors, solution providers and partners to prove that the Cloud is secure.

Security is, of course, the top-most concern for most CIOs when contemplating the movement of sensitive or otherwise high-risk data (customer records, credit card details, etc.) to the Cloud. "We are in the early stages of a fascinating journey into a new computing model that, for all its purported advantages, from a security and risk point of view, is a difficult thing to deal with," says Jay Heiser, an analyst at Gartner. "The things that make it easy and appealing – like the immediate plug-and-play productivity

– also make it impossible to conclusively assess your relative risks."

Standard procedures and best practices for the protection of data are currently in advanced stages of discussion and development, chiefly by working groups of the non-profit Cloud Security Alliance (CSA). All SLAs now incorporate detailed security provisions which clearly enunciate rigidly enforced compliance guidelines and prescribe specific tools for the secure integration of Cloud and non-Cloud resources.

But not all data – and certainly not all high-risk data – even needs to be sent to the Cloud. In fact, at the moment, a hybrid Cloud model makes sense for a good number of organizations. Many firms delegate "outward-facing" apps (tools for collaboration, communications, customer-service, etc.) to Cloud resources, while maintaining sensitive financial and customer data on proprietary servers, or within proprietary private Clouds, behind firewalls. As well, data and apps backups are routinely kept internally.

Yet sometimes the Cloud is the safest place. Cloud providers avail themselves of numerous decentralized data centers across the country and around the world, whereas private data centers tend to be located in a single fixed location, susceptible to hurricanes, earthquakes, and other natural or manmade disasters.

Securing Cloud Computing environments is currently the major focus of all purveyors of Cloud Computing resources. Leading Cloud Computing suppliers are in a race against one another to differentiate themselves by integrating and gaining a reputation for excellence in security. All see this as a key benchmark for long-term success. In turn, security tools vendors who have for so long sold directly to enterprises, now more and more find themselves licensing via Cloud providers who in turn deliver Cloud resources off the shelf to clients with security tools and procedures already baked in.

Cloud Trust Authority's Offerings

The Cloud Trust Authority makes available Identity and Compliance Profiling Services.

Powered by VMware's Project Horizon, the Identity Service is a Cloud-based management service tasked to deliver simple, secure end-user access and provisioning to applications and data across the widest range of end-user devices. The Identity Service is designed to enable a customer to manage secure user access and user provisioning to multiple Cloud providers via federated single sign-on and directory synchronization. The service is engineered using RSA SecurID technology.

The Compliance Profiling Service is engineered to enable customers to view the trust profiles of various Cloud providers against a set of common benchmarks developed by the Cloud Security Alliance. This first-ever Cloud compliance solution is a step towards more automated compliance for Cloud services. By providing centralized access to security profiles of various Cloud providers against a common benchmark, RSA will make it easier for enterprises to rapidly add capabilities and on-board new Cloud service providers, dramatically lowering the barriers to trusted Cloud Computing.

"Security remains top of mind for organizations that wish to leverage the public Cloud more extensively," says Jim Reavis, Executive Director of the Cloud Security Alliance. "The standards and recommendations developed by the Cloud Security Alliance are most effective when they are put into practice by the security industry. RSA has contributed actively to the Cloud Security Alliance standards and was among the first to embrace the Cloud Security Alliance standards within its products. With the RSA Cloud Trust Authority, RSA is taking another decisive step towards delivering comprehensive and innovative solutions for securing the Cloud. The approach of delivering Cloud security services spanning identity, information, and infrastructure will address key concerns that limit the adoption of the Cloud."

"The Cloud Trust Authority is a very strategic investment area for RSA," says Tom Corn, Chief Strategy Officer, RSA (The Security Division of EMC), "one with direct involvement of virtually every technology team across the division. We will be actively engaging with both enterprises and Cloud service providers right away in shaping the future of this solution. Trusted relationships only work with the active engagement of all parties. We see enterprises and service providers as participants in shaping the RSA Cloud Trust Authority. The beta program will lay the foundation for broad-based roll-out of these services."

Common SaaS SLA Pitfalls

SaaS contracts often lack explicit contingency procedures for what is to happen if one or more of the companies involved in a public Cloud suffer a disruption or breach. SLAs must clearly define exactly who is responsible for fixing things in the event of a breakdown of any kind. "It's important we understand there isn't just one Cloud out there. It's about layers of services," says Jim Reavis. "We've seen an evolution where SaaS providers ride atop the other layers, delivered in public and private Clouds. If you're in a public Cloud situation and Company B is breached, a lot of finger pointing between that company and different partners will ensue. If this isn't covered in the terms of agreement up front, you have no hope of recovering data (or damages)."

Security via Hardware

The most robust security in the Cloud comes from, and will continue to come from, hardware rather than software, because the code has not yet been written that cannot be hacked.

For example, Intel's Trusted Execution Technology uses processor-level extensions to create many separate execution environments (partitions), enables secure key generation and storage, and routinely checks the BIOS with every execution in order to notice tampering.

IBM does something along the same lines with its Smarter Planet drive, using chipsets in embedded systems and mobile devices. These chipsets allow for hardware storage of security-related data (keys, certificates, checksums, etc.) and also help facilitate encryption and decryption.

Amazon's "Design for Failure Model"

Amazon's Elastic Compute Cloud 2 (EC2) crashed at 4:41 a.m. Eastern Time on April 21st, 2011. The event took down a number of the Web's most lucrative and heavily-trafficked commercial sites, including Foursquare, Reddit, Cydia, Discovr and Scvngr.

According to *PC World's* Keir Thomas, "the outage was caused by misconfigured mirroring services that filled up all available storage. Inevitable finger-wagging is taking place, with many critics of the Cloud claiming they're vindicated. But it's less of a drama than it might appear. I haven't yet met a computer that wasn't fallible in some way, and I'm not sure why we expect Cloud Computing to be any different. Amazon's uptime has been pretty exceptional otherwise."

The crash proved to be an extended event. "As Amazon's web services outage passed its third day, the debate on the future of Cloud Computing is under way. The outage is costing web sites such as Reddit and Quora considerable losses as users turn elsewhere to get their social media needs met." So wrote Dean Takahashi of the *VentureBeat* blog. "The duration of the outage has surprised many, since Amazon has a lot of backup computing infrastructure. If Amazon can't safeguard the Cloud, how can we rely upon it so? So the debate begins on the future of Cloud Computing and what to do to make users and companies put their trust in Cloud vendors such as Amazon."

"This is a wake-up call for Cloud Computing," Matthew Eastwood, an analyst for IDC, told the *New York Times*. "It will force a conversation in the industry."

O'Reilly's George Reese remains an energetic Cloud booster. "If you think this week exposed weakness in the Cloud, you don't get it: it was the Cloud's shining moment, exposing the strength of Cloud Computing," he wrote. "In short, if your systems failed in the Amazon Cloud this week, it wasn't Amazon's fault. You either deemed an outage of this nature an acceptable risk or you failed to design for Amazon's Cloud Computing model."

The Amazon model is called the "design for failure" model (versus what is known as the "traditional" model). In a "design for failure" approach, which operates in a hybrid paradigm utilizing Iaas, combos of your own software and management tools have the task of maintaining application availability. Thus 100% up-time should be maintainable even if your Cloud provider experiences a data-center-wide disruption.

In a "traditional" model, explains Reese, "the underlying infrastructure takes ultimate responsibility for availability. It doesn't matter how dumb your application is, the infrastructure will provide the redundancy necessary to keep it running in the face of failure. The Clouds that tend to follow this model are vCloud-based Clouds that leverage the capabilities of VMware to provide this level of infrastructural support."

As always, however, the decision on which model to use remains in the hands of the enterprise subscribing to the service, rather than to the service provider. Enterprises which delegate full responsibility to a Cloud provider take the risk of being fully exposed in an event such as occurred at Amazon.

Bottom line: The computer system or network – whether in-house or in the Cloud – has yet to be devised which does not contain the possibility of failure. Cloud economies, meanwhile, remain intact. And the Cloud, when correctly deployed by the subscriber, remains the most secure of all environments as regards systems failure.

Dropbox: The "Problem Child" of Cloud Security?

Dropbox – a leading document-sharing Cloud implementation with some 50 million users worldwide – has recently been called the "problem child" of Cloud security by several leading industry pundits. In an effort to be different, I will simply call it the "poster-child" for Cloud *insecurity*.

In the latter months of 2012, user names and passwords were stolen. Earlier, for a period of about four hours, *all* user files were inexplicably made publicly accessible, and before that hackers discovered a major "security-hole" in the Dropbox iOS app, which (amazingly) stored user log-in information as unencrypted text files.

Dropbox – which says it is targeting individual users rather than the enterprise – nevertheless most certainly has a "trojan horse" strategy of eventually penetrating enterprises simply by the sheer weight and mass of its individual user base. Indeed, thousands of enterprises already use Dropbox, whether they know it or not.

Executives at Dropbox insist (believably) that they are taking swift and robust measures to shore-up the Dropbox firewall and all related security software and procedures. Nevertheless, the recent history of breaches at the firm reveal the types of threats client-firms need to be concerned about when using outside Cloud service providers.

Data Loss Prevention (DLP)

Of course, the beauty of the Cloud model is that it allows users to use powerful apps and extensive data files remotely. There is a grave security risk, however, that users might – accidentally or otherwise – upload sensitive data files or post sensitive information to an insecure environment. Data Loss Prevention (DLP) tools and procedures help guard against such occurrences. (Note: Other phrases used are *Data Leak Protection, Information Loss Prevention* and *Extrusion Prevention.*)

The key element of the DLP paradigm is information (aka, file) tagging – classifying various degrees of data sensitivity, and marking the files according to the defined system. In turn, permissions protocols built into the enterprise system will allow or deny the forwarding and/or uploading of files through various portals, depending on the associated tags.

Simple in concept, DLP is nevertheless quite complex and costly to implement when it comes to the large enterprise. Consider an enterprise with many hundreds of servers on which thousands of directories and tens of thousands of files. Just think of all that tagging. Some of this tagging can be automated. I'm talking about uniformly formatted files such as those containing social security or credit card numbers. But what about the many non-uniform files? What about those containing architectural designs, individual spreadsheets, market forecasts, strategic plans, schematics and the like? These almost always must be tagged "by hand". Of course, another expensive and time-consuming human task within the enterprise is the very definition of the various rules which will be applied for tagging, and the levels of security assigned to various portals.

But regardless of the expense and hassle, DLP is generally worth it when one thinks of the expense and hassles related to data breaches. *Capiche?*

A number of firms offer software solutions to help implement and manage DLP. We are talking about two levels of solutions. Single-channel solutions (S-DLPs) are generally adequate for smaller implementations. Enterprise-solution DLPs, however, are the ones necessary for large enterprises (such as Global 2000 organizations). All viable DLP products focus on three key tasks: monitoring and controlling activity at the endpoint (user-access), filtering data streams on the network, and securing the integrity of "at rest" data.

Firms supplying DLP solutions include Trend Micro, Symantec, Proofpoint, EMC and Zenprise, the latter focusing on mobile data security.

They don't call it the Internet anymore; they call it Cloud Computing. I'm no longer resisting the name. Call it what you want.

- Larry Ellison, Oracle CEO

Author Biography

Lars Nielsen has more than thirty years experience as a systems developer and administrator for a range of *Fortune 500* companies. Nielsen is also the author of New Street's popular *Computing: A Business History* and the bestselling *A Simple Introduction to Data Science*. He resides in Amsterdam.

Call for Authors

New Street is in the process of building a substantial list of publications focused on the interrelated topics of Cloud Computing, Big Data and Data Science. Topics of interest include but are not limited to Hadoop, Cassandra, SQL, Data Modeling, Data Visualization, Big Data tools and techniques, etc. Technologists and consultants with backgrounds in these fields are encouraged to contact us with project proposals. New Street's publications are distributed throughout the United States, Canada, Western Europe, Brazil, India and Japan as both paper- and digital-editions.

Edward Renehan
Managing Director
New Street Communications, LLC
Wickford, RI

ejr@newstreetcommunications.com

About the Publisher

Founded June of 2010, New Street Communications, LLC publishes first-quality nonfiction in a range of fields (also, through Dark Hall Press, first-quality original horror and science fiction). New Street's nonfiction interests include the intersection of digital technology and society; transformative business communication and innovation (particularly the conceptualizing of elegant new tools, markets, products and paradigms); environmental issues; socially-relevant children's literature; travel; and literary criticism. We are located in the seaport town of Wickford, RI, near Newport.

newstreetcommunications.com

20681524R00060

Made in the USA
Lexington, KY
14 February 2013